Drawings from Venice

This exhibition is made possible by major support from Benetton.

Additional support is provided by the Vincent Astor Foundation, British Airways, EniChem Usa, the Howard Gilman Foundation, Instituto Bancario San Paolo di Torino, New York, Manufacturers Hanover Trust Company and The New York Times Company Foundation.

Public funds from the National Endowment for the Arts, the New York State Council on the Arts, and the Institute of Museum Services, a federal agency that offers general operating support to the nation's museums, assist in making this exhibition possible.

This catalogue is made possible in part by a grant from the Samuel H. Kress Foundation.

Published in association with The Drawing Center, New York

Drawings from Venice

Masterworks from the Museo Correr, Venice
Terisio Pignatti & Giandomenico Romanelli

Trefoil Books, London

Published by Trefoil Books Ltd., 7, Royal Parade, Dawes Rd., London SW6 in association with The Drawing Center.

English translation by Simon Rees and Corso Rucellai

ISBN 0 86294 066 4

Published on the occasion of the exhibition 'Drawings from Venice' at The Drawing Center (a nonprofit space for the study and exhibition of drawings), 137 Greene St., New York NY 10012, in April 1985.

Distributed in the United States of America and Canada exclusively by Allanheld & Schram, an imprint of Rowan & Allanheld and Abner Schram Ltd., c/o Biblio Distribution Center, 81 Adans Drive, Totowa, New Jersey 07512.

Set in Plantin Light by Words & Pictures Ltd.
Monochrome printing by BAS Printers Ltd.
Colour printing by Jolly & Barber Ltd.
Binding by Garden City Press Ltd.

Manufactured in the United Kingdom.

Preface

Recorded on the pages of this catalogue, and in the exhibition it celebrates, are glimpses of the long love affair between Venice and her artists – from the admirers' point of view. Connoisseurs of the art of drawing are invited to consider finer questions of attribution and style. The rest of us will be grateful for a breadth of more than three centuries, and for a range that sets the most elaborate formal compositions next to the most spontaneous records of daily life.

Portraits and figure studies, saintly altars and luscious allegories, the view painter's sketch and the architect's project, caricatures and character types, full dress gondoliers and fisher-folk, political pretense and private folly. These fragments, as fragile as loveletters, reflect the vitality and variousness of Venice.

The dedicated efforts of the staffs of the Museo Correr in Venice and the Drawing Center in New York have made this exhibition possible and scholars of Venice have enriched the catalogue. The Samuel H. Kress Foundation is pleased to participate in these endeavours.

Marilyn Perry, President, The Samuel H. Kress Foundation

Foreword

This exhibition celebrates the Drawing Center's eighth anniversary. Since its foundation in 1977, the Center, a nonprofit institution, has sought through exhibitions and educational events to express the diversity, quality and importance of drawing – the creation of unique works on paper – as a major art form. Each year the Center presents five exhibitions. Those of an historical nature such as *Drawings from Venice: Masterworks from the Museo Correr* complement the Center's Selections series – group exhibitions of drawings by promising contemporary artists. It is with special pleasure and pride The Drawing Center presents this exhibition from the Museo Correr in Venice. I would like to thank Terisio Pignatti and Giandomenico Romanelli for selecting the exhibition and preparing the catalogue. Their goodwill, co-operation and generosity have made the exhibition a particularly happy event. I also want to thank our publisher, Conway Lloyd Morgan, for his cheerful help with the catalogue.

The organization of this exhibition was greatly facilitated by the constant support of the Directors of The Drawing Center: Werner H. Kramarsky, Chairman; Mrs. Felix G. Rohatyn, Vice Chairman; Mrs. Walter N. Thayer, Vice Chairman; James M. Clark, Jr.; George R. Collins; Mrs. Colin Draper; Colin Eisler; William S. Lieberman; Francis S. Mason, Jr.; Mrs. Gregor W. Medinger; Douglas Newton and Edward H. Tuck. We also appreciate the contribution of our Advisory Committee: Egbert Haverkamp-Begeman; Per Bjurgström; Dennis Farr; John Harris and C. Michael Kauffmann. Special thanks go to my colleagues Elinore Antell, Director of Development, Peter Gilmore, Exhibition Assistant, Marie T. Keller, Associate Curator, and Michael Moran, Administrative Assistant. All of us thank the many work/study students and interns who have made our tasks easier and more pleasurable.

Finally, I would like to thank the following people who have helped in innumerable ways:
Pierre Apraxine, Mrs. Vincent Astor, Mrs. Donald Blinken, Huntington T. Block, Sukey Bryan, Keith Davis, Hon. Giulio C. di Lorenzo, Alfredo di Marzio, Suzanne M. Flaton, Mrs. Gianluigi Gabetti, Carlo E. Gallone, Linda Gillies, Howard Gilman, Lucien Goldschmidt, Mrs. Marco Grassi, Sydney Gruson, Fred M. Heckinger, Laura Hillyer, James B. Hurlock, Michael Iovenko, John Lampl, Peter Laundy, Colin Marshall, John d'A. Meredith, Chris and John Millerchip, Ward Mintz, Natalie Moody, Mary Moro, Laura Neagle, Andrew Oliver, Davide Paolini, Meg Pearlman, Marilyn Perry, Piero Stucchi Prinetti, Janet Riker, Gilbert Robinson, Felix G. Rohatyn, David Rosand, Sarah Rubenstein, Claudio Scoretti, James. B. Sherwood, Leslie Spector, Harry Taylor, Brenda Trimarco, A. Richard Turner, and Lella and Massimo Vignelli.

Martha Beck
Director, The Drawing Center

Contents

(Note that the works illustrated in Prof. Pignatti's article are not included in the exhibition)

THEODORVS CORRERIVS
PATRICIVS VENETVS
Natus Anno CIƆIƆCCL.

1795

Bernardino Castelli pin. Vincentius Giaconi inc.

Introduction

*Giandomenico
Romanelli*

The collection of drawing seen by the present-day visitor to the Museo Correr is the result of a gradual accumulation, over the last one hundred years or more, of works from different private collections, each of them interesting and original but having in common the quality of conveying special moments and events and important personalities in the history of Venetian art in its widest sense.

Each group of drawings thus reflects in its own way the taste, cultural attitudes and opportunities of the original collector, and testify to the conditions under which the collection was put together. Thus the special value of the collection of Teodoro Correr we owe to his fortunate acquisition of their fathers' drawings from Francesco Guardi's sons Giacomo and Pietro Longhi's sons Giacomo and Alessandro; and the precious album of drawings from Leopoldo Cicognara's collection is a tribute to the friendship between him and various Neoclassical artists, beginning with Canova, attested by the dedications on most of the drawings and their singular quality.

The Correr catalogue comprises more than eight thousand identified drawings, covering a considerable time-span, but principally concentrating on the period beteen the late fifteenth century and the early nineteenth, and with a special breadth of scope and quality for the eighteenth century. It would be by no means unreasonable to suggest that the Correr is the most varied of the present collections of Venetian drawings, a fact underlined by the real importance and broad sweep of the Correr's eighteenth-century holdings, despite a single major lack, the absence of more than a single work by Canaletto. However, it is true that he was quite insufficiently represented as a *vedutista* in Venetian collections until a year ago, when the Musei Civici acquired two early works, showing the rio dei Mendicanti and the Grand Canal from St Toma to the Rialto (Canaletto's drawings are well represented, in the Cini Foundation and in the Accedemia, which contains the famous Cagnola book of sketches).

Turning to the Correr's own collection, it is worth asking how and why it began, or rather what was its source. Teodoro Correr was one of those collectors who can properly be called omnivorous and insatiable. He began buying as soon as he came of age; despite an appointment as an abbé he let slip all public duties and any ordinary private life to give himself wholeheartedly to his zeal as a collector. The descendant of an old Venetian family, his own inheritance was certainly not great, but he had the good fortune — at least in posterity's terms — to be in the right place at the right moment, at the heart of a market panic which affected many of the largest, richest and best-endowed private collections. For after the fall of the Venetian Republic in 1797 many noble Venetian families — through hardship, fear of confiscation or the need for cash, from stupidity or short-sightedness — wished to break up their collections of secular works of art. Much that was sold in the eighteenth century found its way into foreign collections. Of what had escaped, much came onto the market in the 1810s. Teodoro Correr was able to fill his house at San Zandelogà with treasures of all sorts: paintings, antique and modern statues, coins and medals, illuminated manuscripts and books, gems and cameos and, above all, drawings.

Very often these drawings would not be the normal stuff of amateur collectors, those very finished and prestigious drawings, made by painters with collectors and dilettanti in mind, which, because of their importance and quality can be considered as substitutes for paintings. Rather, Correr acquired sketches, working drawings and studio studies. But not infrequently there is no denying, such workshop drawings can make a crucial contribution to our knowledge of an artist and so to his critical reputation, or can help to fill the serious gaps that may exist in our judgement of the dating or attribution of particular paintings.

No less important are the various collection of architectural and ornamental drawings that have found their way at various times into the collection of the Museum. There is the fundamental collection of Neoclassical drawings which we owe to the architect and professor Giannantonio Selva, and the huge series of Baroque drawings, known as the *album Gaspari*, after the follower of Baldessare Longhena whose studio continued that tradition. There are architectural studies in

9

Vincenzo Scamozzi's own hand, as well as drawings, made in the eighteenth and nineteenth centuries, documenting a large number of Venetian buildings, some of which have been subsequently demolished.

In the nineteenth century — in common with the development of the principal Italian museums, particularly of municipal museums, the collections of the Correr, of paintings, drawings, and other works of art, continued to be enriched by gifts and donations. Often these were of the highest quality, but they also often served as a clear guide to the taste, culture and interests of donors, and often their passion for historical documents, especially related to issues of national interests. From such enthusiasms the Correr acquired the major collection of Bartolomeo Gamba, and later those of Girolamo Ascanio Molin, Domenico Zoppetti (in 1852), Emmanuele Cicogna (1865), Eugenio Bosa (1876), Francesco Wcovich Lazzari (1886) and Giuseppe Gatteri, with its famous Tiepolo album, in 1885. In the present century this generous tradition has been continued by Morosini, Caffi, Sullam, Musatti, Morassi and others.

Each of these collections is by its nature the reflection of the culture, tastes and opportunities of the collector in question: so some can be seen as reactionary others ahead of their times, while others portray exactly the tastes and aspirations of their era.

To these groups of drawings must be added individual drawings, acquired either in the marketplace or from private individuals. These have added to the richness, variety and diversity of the Museum's holdings.

In effect the Museo Correr cannot be said to lack masterworks, as indeed this exhibition bears witness: indeed several hundred more interesting and important drawings could have been selected, had space permitted. The history of art in Venice and the Veneto cannot, today, be appreciated without taking note of the Correr, witness the frequent inclusion, in recent decades, of works from the Museum in monographs on important artists, in general works of art history, and in exhibitions of paintings and drawings worldwide.

Acknowledgements

The Director of the Civic Museums of Venice wants to thank the Soprintendenza ai Beni Culturali, of Venice, whose Head, Dr. Francesco Valcanover has greatly helped in all the procedure for organizing this exhibition. Grateful thanks are also due to Dr. Attilia Dorigato, of the Correr Museum Library, for collecting the drawings; to Dr. Filippo Pedrocco, of the Civic Museums, for preparing the Bibliography; to Miss Margherita Giacometti, for research and translation of most of the entries; to Domenico Falconera and the staff of the Correr Museum.

Special thanks are also due to Mrs. Laura Morassi, for securing to the exhibition the two precious drawings by Gian Antonio Guardi and Bellotto, on temporary loan to the Correr Museum.

Giandomenico Romanelli
Director, Correr Museum

Venetian Drawing 1400-1800

Terisio Pignatti

The interest shown in Venetian drawing by the present generation of scholars has certainly led to remarkable progress in our knowledge. It therefore seems reasonable to give at least a brief summary of the subject, as an introduction to the best of a collection of drawings which is essentially concerned with the work of artists in Venice and the Veneto between the earliest times and the eighteenth century.

What can be termed the language of early Venetian drawing often tends to avoid the rules that characterise this artistic genre in other Italian circles. Four centuries of Venetian graphic tradition might be summed up in the motto *fare, del disegno, pittura* [to make a painting of a drawing].

Moreover, right from the time of the early mosaics in San Marco, colour seems to have been destined to prevail in Venice over drawing: thus, a summary pictoricism is contrasted with the sculptural arrangement of masses in the figures. While critics in the Tuscan tradition of the Cinquecento would discuss drawing according to linear and sculptural values, as opposed to what they considered the equivocal suggestions of Titianesque colour, in Venice the art of drawing is closer to the art of painting: this effectively cancelled any artificial distinctions on the technical level, and a unifying vision established itself among artists who practiced it.

We can identify a further elements, that links the most disparate Venetian drawings: this is their general independence from the process of creating other works of art. Unlike most artists of other schools or countries, a Venetian rarely conceives drawing as merely an element in planning a project. That is to say he does not consider it solely preparatory: instead, he uses his graphic imagination with remarkable independence — just as he approaches works of greater technical difficulty, on canvas or in fresco. Each sketch therefore tends to be a work of art in itself, in which the formal spirit of the painting, which would often be produced after it, is already hinted at or expressed.

One confirmation of the creative nature of Venetian drawing is to be found in the remarkably high estimation in which it was held by writers on art, by collectors and by artists themselves. One finds nothing comparable to this attitude in Tuscany and Rome. From the middle of the sixteenth century one can follow the development of an aesthetic battle fought between the Venetian critics and the others, especially those of Tuscany and Rome. The latter argued doggedly for the superiority of line, which the Tuscans conceived to be a way of evaluating plastic effects, over colour, considered by such as Vasari, Pino and Dolce to be a fundamental element in painting, as was to be shown, for instance, in the works of Titian.

The age-old controversy between Tuscans and Venetians has been revived in modern criticism. The writings of Berenson, Degenhart, Hadeln and the Tietzes often start from an evaluation that distinguishes between an essentially linear graphic art, with a tendency towards sculptural effect, and the more summary and unplanned idiom, inspired by the freer pictorial art of the Venetians. The fact is that the Venetians were above all interested in drawing as an independent artistic genre, on a level with the most initimate creations of figurative poetry, reducing to a minimum the matter of planning that remains much more in evidence in other cultural circles. This outcome is probably connected with a particular Venetian tendency towards a pictorial style of drawing, sketched rapidly, directly and briskly. Colour in Venice comes to prevail over delineated form, and this element in the Venetian idiom is always reflected in drawing, during the four centuries in its development of which we will now trace a brief outline.

With the exception of those illustrations that often appear in Mediaeval manuscripts, the earliest Venetian drawings date back to the end of the fourteenth century. Among these, we have the evidence of a few graphic notes left by Lorenzo Veneziano on the back of his polyptych of 1359, now in the Gallerie di Venezia. The fifteenth century abounds in drawings by such masters of the International Gothic as Gentile da Fabriano and Maestro Stefano, and later the great Pisanello (Fig. 1). It is remarkable, however, that these artists are only marginally concerned with the

1. Antonio Pisanello (*c.* 1395-1455/6)
Head of a woman
Louvre, Paris

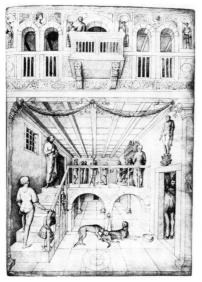

2. Jacopo Bellini (*c.* 1400-70/1)
The Head of Hannibal presented to the King of
Bithynia
Louvre, Paris

3. Andrea Mantegna (*c.* 1431-1506)
The Descent into the tomb
Lehman collection

4. Giovanni Bellini (*c.* 1430-1516)
The Martyrdom of St James
Donnington Priory

capital, preferring the areas of Lombardy and Verona. The enormous influence of
this school should not be underestimated. It was consolidated by the transmission
of books of drawings belonging to a succession of artists, who added drawings of
their own (Fossi, 1966).

The first generation fifteenth-century Venetians left very little, and there is not
much we can be sure about in the tiny catalogue of drawings by Giambono and
Antonio Vivarini. But the results achieved by their school are important, as we can
see from Jacopo Bellini's famous *Libri di disegni*, now kept in the British Museum
and the Louvre (Fig. 2). Although it is doubtful whether all the drawings in those
collections are from the hand of Bellini himself, insofar as the hands of his sons
Gentile and Giovanni have recently been recognised, they served as one of the
bases for the revival of a typically Venetian style of drawing in the second half of the
fifteenth century (Tietze, 1944; Canova, 1972).

However, the influence of Tuscan culture was increasing at the same time in
Padua, brought there by Florentines such as Lippi, Uccello and Donatello. A
drawing by Pollaiolo, in fact, is mentioned among the material in the studio of
Squarcione, who was the founder and organiser of the new Paduan school. And it is
not hard to prove that the drawings of Andrea Mantegna — the most relevant of the
artists working in Padua in the fourteen-fifties and sixties — owe something to
Florentine models, both in drawing and engraving (Fig. 3). Mantegna assumed a
very influential position over his contemporaries, both in painting and drawing, as
we can see from the drawings of Marco Zoppo, as well as those of Crivelli,
Bartolomeo Vivarini and of the Ferraresi themselves (Paccagnini, 1961). But
where a critical problem arises is in the difficulty of recognising the early drawings
of Giovanni Bellini, who was a strict follower of Mantegna in the years of his
inspiration by Donatello. There has been an argument for some time between those
who tend to restrict the catalogue of Bellini's drawings to a few sheets, mostly from
his later period, which are certainly from his hand, and those who enlarge the
catalogue to include other examples formerly ascribed to Mantegna, and basing
their arguments on a drawing in Donnington Priory (Fig. 4) connected to the
Mantegnesque *Martyrdom of St James* in the Eremitani, regard its style as the
graphical forerunner of the young Bellini (Robertson, 1968).

Actually Gentile Bellini's style of drawing seems to be initially inspired by the
ceremonial and broadly perspective manner of his father Jacopo. Later on, in his
portraits and record drawings, it tends towards a naturalistic realism that would
partly be taken up by Carpaccio. But first we should consider the whole group of
artists whose central figure, in various ways, was Antonello da Messina, who was in
Venice in 1485-86 — a milestone in the development of Venetian painting in the

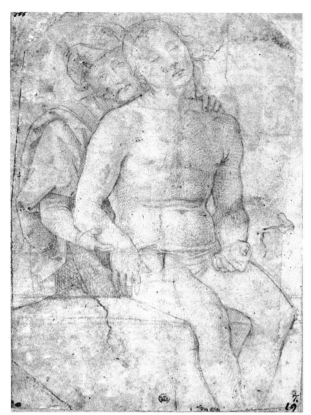

5. Jacopo de'Barbari (*c.* 1445-*c.* 1515)
Pietà
Nationalmuseum, Stockholm

6. Vittore Carpaccio (*c.* 1460/5-1523/6)
Head of a young man
Christchurch, Oxford

Quattrocento. Little or nothing is known about Antonello's drawings. Certain portraits (such as that in the Albertina) are ascribed to him more by tradition than by anything else, and these follow the scheme of panel-paintings (Fiocco, 1951). But after Antonello's time traces of his profoundly incisive teaching were to be found in the work of Alvise Vivarini, Montagna, Cima and Basaiti: their rare drawings sometimes moreover seem to show traces of the style of Mantegna in their marked chiaroscuro (Tietze, 1944).

Albrecht Dürer's presence in Venice in 1494 and again in 1505 (Panofsky, 1948) was another factor which directed the last generation of Quattrocento painters towards this type of technique, involving a careful attention to reality. Dürer introduced a realistic technique which was until then unknown to the Venetians. Among other things, he exerted a direct influence upon Jacopo de' Barbari, a Venetian who had almost certainly returned from a visit to Nuremburg, and who apparently later became the master who taught the Renaissance manner to the Germans. His extremely rare drawings (in the British Museum and in Stockholm; Fig. 5), as well as his famous woodcut of the Map of Venice of 1500 demonstrate this influence clearly (Pignatti, 1964).

Dürer's lessons, together with the influence of Bellini, were also relevant factors in the complex training of Vittore Carpaccio (Fig. 6). About fifty drawings of various types are usually ascribed to him, from general sketches to particularized details; they were evidently drawn from the life, and are astonishing in their pictorial freedom and their graphic inspiration, which in certain cases achieves authentically picturesque effects (Pignatti, 1972; Muraro, 1978).

In turning to consider the Cinquecento, we cannot unfortunately give more than a few brief indications of its first great protagonist, Giorgione. Among the many

7. Giorgione (c. 1476/8-1510)
Shepherd boy
Museum Boymans van Beuningen, Rotterdam

8. Titian (c. 1487/90-1576)
Two Satryrs
Baer collection

drawings said to be from his hand, we can only be absolutely certain about the *Shepherd Boy* in Rotterdam (Fig. 7), which is oddly restrained and not in the least revolutionary — unlike his paintings; in its technique it stands somewhere between Bellini and Dürer. However, in other drawings attributed to him, like the *Saint's Head* in a private collection in Zurich, the almost excessive influence of his young and gifted competitor Titian is apparent (Pignatti, 1978).

At the beginning of the sixteenth century, Titian's personality had made itself noticed in drawing as it had already done in painting, in absolutely independent ways. To appreciate this, one need only compare the restrained but intense expression of the drawings of subjects that are still Giorgionesque, such as that of the Baer *Satyrs* (Fig. 8), with the more archaising drawings by Giulio Campagnola, or of Sebastiano del Piombo and Palma the Elder themselves (Oberhauer, 1976; Rearick, 1976). In any case, we cannot explain Titian simply by means of local comparisons, however diverse and varied. His graphic brilliance, also expressed in the field of woodcuts with his *Triumph of Christ* or the latter *Crossing of the Red Sea*, can only be compared with that of Dürer (Pignatti, 1973). In the first decade of the sixteenth century, when the young Titian began his artistic career, Dürer's large woodcuts of the *Apocalypse* and his first engravings on metal may in fact have already been familiar in Venice: they also influenced Giorgione, who often used them as the source for backgrounds and details in his paintings. We can regularly detect Dürer's stylistic influence, rather than direct references to objects portrayed, in Titian's drawings. It is not merely a question of villages with sloping roofs, towers or castles of a Nordic flavour, or bleak or grandly-forested mountains, but above all Dürer's influence shows in violence of handling, with lines scratched as if with a claw, in search of real light (Pignatti-Chiari, 1979). In his later technique, Titian was to revert to the Roman sculptural style, which leaves its mark on the few surviving drawings of his maturity (the contents of his studio were lost in 1576, during the plague in which Titian himself was to die). These drawings show the same opening-up that can be seen in his late, evocative painting. The problem of the many Titianesque landscape-drawings remains a subject for debate, and many critics have focused their doubts upon them. Many drawings traditionally attributed to him are actually by Domenico Campagnola, an incisive draughtsman who made landscape-drawing his speciality (Oberhuber, 1976).

Pordenone's drawing is linked to Titian's mature phase: many of his drawings are known, ranging from sketches for cartoons to drawings that are freer in composition, such as the *Magdalene* in Princeton (Fig. 9) or the stupendous

9. Giovanni Antonio da Pordenone (1483-1539)
St Mary Magdalene
The Art Museum, Princeton University

10. Andrea Schiavone (1522-63)
Psyche presented to the gods
Metropolitan Museum of Art, New York

11. Lorenzo Lotto (*c.* 1480-1556)
Madonna
Gabinetto Nazionale, Rome

Crucifixion in the Morgan Library (Cohen, 1980). Compared to Titian's freedom of handling, they show a more controlled and intellectualized structure, their inspiration being more central-Italian than Venetian. Romanino, who came from Brescia but was trained in Venice in the post-Giorgione circle, was another artist who had some points in common with this style of drawing, and there are many fine examples of his work in the Gardner Museum and in the Scholz Collection. His drawings show a fluttering and airy touch, with a decorative talent that is astonishingly in advance of his time. Paris Bordone, who followed Titian in his manner of painting, often approaches Romanino in his graphic style. His figure-drawings are often confused with those of the Brescian, Savoldo, whose sketches of heads are often developed from Titianesque suggestions; but attempts at assigning landscape drawings to him have been unsuccessful (Canova, 1963). Schiavone deserves to be remembered among the draughtsmen of the mid-sixteenth century. He fulfilled an important function in making the graphic taste displayed in Parmigianino's prints accessible, and often copied them in chiaroscuro drawings with an elaborate pen and wash technique (Fig. 10 — Richardson, 1980).

We have recently learned more about the drawings of Lotto, and about twenty can now be ascribed to him with certainty (Pouncey, 1965). The *Madonna* in the Gabinetto Nazionale in Rome, and the *Female Head* in the Gallerie di Venezia, were produced in his early period when he was influenced by Dürer's graphic style, and they are handled and engraved in the same manner as the paintings he produced before 1508. The beautiful *Martyrdom* the National Gallery of Washington and the *Martyrdom of St Lucia* in the Hofer collection in Cambridge, may be connected to his Bergamo phase. The identification of the *Holy Family* in the British Museum, and other later discoveries in Paris and London, have allowed the narrative and realistic style of drawing of his mature period to be evaluated (Fig. 11).

Recent studies have also re-assessed the drawings of Jacopo Bassano, many of which were found in his studio after his death, and increased the catalogue of his known output to almost a hundred works (Rearick, 1962; Ballarin, 1969-73). Jacopo Bassano shows links with the sources of German engraving in his early works in pencil or pen, but his later medium was black chalk, often heightened with white or coloured chalks on bluish or grey paper (Fig. 12). Typical of this are the *Apostles' heads* in Vienna and in the Scholz collection, and the sheets in Princeton, the Uffizi and the Louvre. Bassano shows the utmost diligence in the pictorial technique of these drawings, and produces luminous effects through retracing in charcoal and highlighting. The drawings of Francesco Bassano, who had a long and anonymous collaboration with his father, are often difficult to identify. They are characterised, however, by a more fluid and imprecise line, but are, in effect,

INTRODUCTION

12. Jacopo Bassano (c. 1510/18-92)
E.B. Crocker Art Gallery

13. Jacopo Tintoretto (1518-94)
Male nude
Ashmolean Museum, Oxford

I Albrecht Dürer
Madonna
See no. 2, p. 49

minutely-detailed genre-pictures. Many drawings are attributed to Bassano's other son, Leandro, and the most typical of these are the *Portraits*, such as the one in Oxford, which are realistic and insistent in line. The more descriptive and incisive of these, however, are often now attributed to Carletto Caliari (Ballarin, 1971; Oberhuber, 1973).

About fifty of the hundred and thirty-odd drawings attributed to Tintoretto are certainly from his hand, since they are connected to paintings that are positively by him, above all those drawings in the Uffizi, the Louvre and the Lehman collection in New York (Rossi, 1975). Ridolfi notes that Tintoretto often used to draw casts of antique sculpture in order to study their plastic effect, positioning them so as to obtain a contrast between light and shade, much as he also used a sort of puppet-theatre, lit artificially. Very few of his drawings illustrate complete compositions: the other drawings are of isolated figures, almost always nude (Fig. 13). The reason for this choice may be found in the artist's Mannerist training: he intended his drawing to have an independent function, as Ridolfi records, it was not merely intended to serve as a study from nature.

The question of Tintoretto's juvenile drawings has recently been brought to the attention of scholars. These drawings undoubtedly include a group of studies of Michelangelesque and classicial sculptures, dating from the fifteen-fifties and now in the Uffizi, Christ Church, Munich and the Morgan Library. Tintoretto's late drawings are restricted to an evocative outline, full of a restrained energy that is ready to burst the limits of the flexible and broken strokes.

The similarity of Domenico Tintoretto's style of drawing to that of his father Jacopo has long affected his catalogue of works, and we have only recently managed to identify the works of the son. At the basis of this work of reattribution was the recognition that the sketchbook in the British Museum, with its ninety drawings in oil and charcoal heightened in white, resembling other examples in Princeton, is in Domenico's hand (Tietze, 1944). Characteristic of Domenico's art is its narrative

II Ercole de'Roberti
Battle Scene
See no. 1, p. 49

III Jacopo Bassano
Adoration of the Shepherds
See no. 5, p. 21

IV Vincenzo Scamozzi
Design for a Tomb
See no. 11, p. 56

V Gian Battista Tiepolo
Sketch of a Female Head
See no. 69, p. 98

VI Francesco Maffei
Man in Armour
See no. 15, p. 59

21

VII Giuseppe Bernardino Bison
Hurdy-gurdy Players and Countrywomen
See no. 117, p. 136

VII Gerolamo Mauro
Study for a Festival Bissona
See no. 45, p. 82

VIII Francesco Zuccarelli
Landscape with Peasants
See no. 76, p. 104

14. Palma il Giovane (1544-1628)
The Entombment of Christ
Art Institute of Chicago

IX Jacopo Guarana
Venus Triumphant
See no. 37, p. 77

15. Paolo Veronese (*c*. 1528-88)
Head of a woman
Art Institute of Chicago

basis, and its tendency towards close realism: the evocative *Female Figure* in the Ames Collection in Saunderstown is a typical example.

Palma the Younger's catalogue of drawings is chiefly composed of the collection of 134 sheets in the British Museum, two books of 223 and 252 leaves in Munich and others in the Louvre, the Albertina and the Uffizi. There are many other examples in the United States, with collections of drawings in Chicago, the Morgan Library, the Fogg Museum and the Metropolitan, etc. (Mason Rinaldi, 1973). Palma the Younger showed an exceptional talent in the abundance, the variety and the quality of his drawings, which he produced in Venice from 1568 onwards, after his return from Rome (Mason Rinaldi, 1983). His early drawings show a close adherence to the style of Titian, or at least to that of Bassano, a link that is also shown in his use of black chalk heightened with white. The artist's character found greater freedom of expression in the pages of the sketchbooks, which he filled with a dizzying range of sketches of figures in different postures, drawn with different techniques, mostly in pen. In his more elaborate drawings, Palma used wash to produce chiaroscuro effects of light and shade, sometimes adding gold highlights on a dark ground, as in the fine *Entombment of Christ* in Chicago (Fig. 14).

Veronese's career as a draughtsman developed in parallel to that of Tintoretto and his follwers, but in an independent manner. He produced a huge number of drawings, among them, in the family inventory of 1682, some 94 chiaroscuro studies, 126 charcoals, 620 sketches in pen and black chalk, and 646 other designs and various small preparatory drawings (Cocke, 1973-77; Pignatti, 1976). Even though he was familiar with the results achieved by Titian, Bassano and Tintoretto, Veronese's drawing tends chiefly towards the Mannerist style of the Emilian school, also found in the work of Schiavone: the way he illuminates the chiaroscuros, as in the *Allegory of Victory* in Vienna, is indeed very close to these sources. In his pen sketches, Veronese uses a typically disordered line, which he treats with an impulsive and Manneristic flexibility. Other chiaroscuro drawings of figures and heads in black chalk on tinted paper, like those in Chicago or the Lehman collection, are heightened in white chalk with an especially striking effect (Fig. 15).

From the work of Tintoretto, Bassano and Veronese, we move on to the seventeenth century. Until very recently, the study of seventheenth-century drawing has remained at a rudimentary level (Ivanoff, 1959; Pignatti, 1959). The long silence of scholarship in this area has undoubtedly caused the work of many remarkably skilful graphic artists to be unjustly neglected. It is obvious that, thanks to the arrival of foreign artists who contributed the fruits of their new experience, the academic crisis into which Venetian art had been plunged after two centuries of uninterrupted glory, came to be resolved in the second decade of the seventeenth century. But Caravaggio's influence hardly affected Venice itself, but became localized, if anywhere, in Verona, where Bassetti returned after a four-year visit to Rome between 1616 and 1620. The influence of Caravaggio is shown in Bassetti's many drawings, in ink-wash or in oil on prepared paper. Those in the Royal Collection at Windsor are particularly important, and show the effects of his Roman experience in their strongly-contrasted lighting (Blunt–Croft-Murray, 1957).

Caravaggio's influence is less evident in the work of Domenico Fetti, a Roman painter who arrived in Venice from Mantua between 1620 and 1621. Some preparatory sketches for well-known works, such as the drawings for the Mantua *Trinity* in the Schwarz collection in Larchmont, New York, have recently been attributed to Fetti, and this has been the most relevant point in the reconstruction of his graphic œuvre. Fetti's sketching shows a fluent style, obviously adopted in Venice, that can even be confused with that of Tintoretto. Other important drawings show Rubens's inspiration on the artist in his Mantuan period, in their undulating *pastoso* handling.

John Liss of Oldenburg, who arrived in Venice in 1621, was another person who found inspiration in Rubens. He also recalls Fetti in some of his drawings, and Liss is known to have admired him during their stay in Venice. About ten drawings are

INTRODUCTION

16. Johann Liss (*c.* 1597-1629/30)
Allegory of Faith
Cleveland Museum of Art

17. Bernardo Strozzi (1581-1644)
Head of a woman
Suida-Manning collection

certainly from his hand, and these allow us to form a precise idea of his style: it is
airy and light in his pen and ink technique, as can be seen from his signed drawing in
Cleveland (Fig. 16), while in his pen or charcoal drawings his style is brilliant and
full of the spirit of Callot (Exhibition catalogue, 1975).

The third major figure in the renewal of Venetian painting at the beginning of the
seventeenth century is the Genoese, Bernardo Strozzi, who produced a vast,
delightful and idiosyncratic collection of drawings (Mortari, 1966). We have only
recently learned about his early drawings, which consist of group, now mainly in
the Civic Collections in Genoa, inspired by the styles of Salimbeni and Sorri, the
young painter's master in Siena. In these drawings, Strozzi had not yet adopted the
sfumato technique of black or red chalk which was to become his characteristic.
Instead, he continues to use a pungently Manneristic line, building up his figures by
means of variable masses of shading, under violet lighting. Strozzi's later Genoese
drawings and those of his Venetian period (from 1630 to 1644) are hard to tell apart.
Some very find Heads, such as the one in the Manning collection in New York
(Fig. 17) which is close to the softly-treated *Figure of a Female Saint* in Cleveland, are

18. Francesco Maffei (*c.* 1600-1660)
Figure of a warrior
Museo Correr, Venice

19. Giulio Carpioni (1611-1674)
Bacchus punishing the Maenads for the death of Orpheus
Private collection

related to Venetian styles by their silvery and luminous colouring in the manner of Veronese. Other brilliant drawings are of the Gennese Bermerdo Stzozzi, who reached Venice in 1633.

Although Francesco Maffei was a very well-known and prolific painter, only a few drawings from his hand can be identified (Ivanoff, 1942). The drawing of an *Apostle* in the Bassano Museum can only be connected with a very late work, while other figure-compositions recently recognised in the Carrara Academy in Bergamo leave us in uncertainty. The fiery *Figure of a Warrior* in the Correr Museum (Fig. 18) is perhaps the most firmly attributed. Because of his passion for painting, it is supposed that Maffei made few drawings: if this could ever be proved, it would be a surprising fact, especially as he was the pupil of so prolific a draughtsman as Maganza of Vicenza, who left numerous sketches, including those in the Scholz collection in New York.

Among the second generation of seventeenth-century artists, we know some examples of Pietro Vecchia's drawings. He was an unpredictable artist in every sense, with his unique, even grotesque treatement of his subjects and his daring handling of pen and wash, shown in the drawings in the Correr, in Sacramento and in the collection of Janos Scholz (Pignatti, 1959). Carpioni left many drawings in the variety of techniques, pen, pencil and charcoal, also in the Correr, that are much more restrained, even to the point of Classicism. Carpioni was a unique personality in the culture of eighteenth-century Venice, being in the tradition of the Bolognese classicism of Domenichino and Albani. he is also connected, in the field of drawing, with the Bolognese, Cantarini (Pilo, 1961). He was certainly familiar with Testa's prints, and these brought him close to a subject-matter and to certain styles that are clearly derived from Poussin. Carpioni stands in an important position, where his drawings are concerned as well as his prints. Consider especially how much a genius of Tiepolo's mental capacity owed to him. In the century that followed, Tiepolo recalls more of Carpioni's manner than might be expected: his fresh, sharp luminosity of line and the unprejudiced and prophetic use he makes in his drawing of the chromatic effects of areas of white were to offer many suggestions of idiom to the Venetian draughtsmen of the eighteenth century (Fig. 19).

Mazzoni's drawings are too little known for anyone to risk a judgement on his stature as a draughtsman. Many sheets of pastel drawings, like those in the Louvre, which used to be attributed to him as early works, are now being ascribed instead to Tuscan artists such as Furini and Cecco Bravo, while the attribution to him of pen-drawings such as the *Saint* in the Uffizi, or the *Eucharist* in a private collection, remains hypothetical, although quite likely (Muraro, 1953).

The *tenebrosi* painters were responsible for the flourishing of Venetian drawing in the last quarter of the seventeenth century. We know for certain some examples of drawings by the German painter, Carl Loth. Often using a broken line, he adopts Bassetti's chiaroscuro style and characteristic techniques (Ewald, 1965). Zanchi, a master who carried on working into the first decades of the eighteenth century, also left some drawings, including the *Coronation of the Doge* now in the Los Angeles County Museum and *Chronos* in the Cooper Hewitt Museum. Some drawings have now been added to the few previously attributed to the Friulian painter Carneo; the most important is the one formerly in the Weinmüller Collection, and now in the List Collection in Munich (Rizzi, 1960). Lastly, some remarkable progress has been made in research into Celesti's drawings, and the drawing in Chicago for the painting formerly in the Ascensione in Venice can now be attributed to him, besides those in the Correr. These demonstrate his remarkable importance in the formation of the *chiarista* style that became predominant at the beginning of the eighteenth century and aided the coming of the Rococo style in figure-painting (Pignatti, 1980).

Venetian painting entered one of its most favourable periods in the eighteenth century, and many artists of genius flourished in a particularly receptive cultural and social environment. The various travelling painters are typical of the initial period.

20. Sebastiano Ricci (1659-1734)
Rebecca at the well
Accademia, Venice

From the early decades of the century, the two Riccis, Pellegrini, Amigoni and Diziani spent time in Rome, Naples, Florence and Milan, and later in England, the Low Countries, France, Germany and Poland. It is natural that their style of drawing fits into a wider international experience, rather than concentrating closely on the themes developed in late seventeenth-century Venice and the Veneto.

It was Sebastiano Ricci (Fig. 20) who effected the transition from late Baroque to Rococo. His first drawings, dating from the last years of the seventeenth century, clearly show their origin in the tradition established by the Carraccis, and his use of the styles of Giordano and Solimena recalls his experience in Naples. Traces of this training were to remain until he broadened his plastic style into an increasingly sonorous and decorative Rococo way of drawing, that established him as one of the most successful draughtsmen of his time, as the albums of his drawings at Windsor and the Gallerie di Venezia show (Rizzi, 1975).

There is a close rapport between Ricci's drawings and those of Giovanni Antonio Pellegrini, who wished to surpass the limits of the seventeenth-century plastic tradition in painting as in drawing, and moved towards a personal conception of open forms which marks the transition between the styles of the Baroque and the Rococo. A large group of early drawings in the Düsseldorf Museum, previously attributed to the seventeenth-century painter Molinari, have been ascribed to this period of Pellegrini's work (Bettagno, 1959). Later, with his experience in Rome of Baciccio's free and vigorous drawings, Pellegrini was able to develop his style of edged forms that are open to the light: the *Saint in Glory* in the Scholz collection in New York is the best example of this style (Fig. 21). Pellegrini's basic experience

matured through his journey to England between 1708 and 1713, where he came
into contact with the work of Rembrandt and Van Dyck. Pellegrini used new
themes gained from both of them to enrich his style of drawing, basing it on a very
individual feeling for mottled effects, with variegated lighting and agile touches of
contour. Later, he went to the Low Countries and Germany, where his interest in
Dutch and Flemish painting increased still further: indeed, his drawings for the
Mauritshuis in the Hague seem to be thorough-going Venetian versions of
Rembrandt. This tendency in his work was later to be fundamental to Tiepolo's
development. Pellegrini's later drawings show quite graphic rarefaction and a
dazzling luminosity, and it is here, as in the drawings in the Philadelphia Museum
and the Dresden Collection, and the *Adoration of the Magi* in Leningrad that his style
is seen to be of importance to the training of Antonio Guardi.

The early drawings of the elder of the Guardi brothers probably date from
around 1730, and it is almost possible to confuse them with the open style of
Pellegrini, as in the *Aurora* in the Spector collection, New York (Fig. 22). He also
demonstrates this manner in his numerous drawings of the *Fasti Veneziani*, derived
from the historical paintings in the Doge's Palace: there are examples of these in the
Cini Foundation albums, and in the unbound drawings in Cleveland, St. Louis and
Minneapolis. His last drawings are wonderfully airy and decorative, and are
connected to paintings like the Cini *Aurora* and the *Angel Raphael*. In the Correr
Museum, and in various other collections, he reaches the height of the aetherial and
dancing style of the Rococo (Morassi, 1975; Pignatti, 1983).

Jacopo Amigoni, an artist of international fame and activity throughout the first
fifty years of the eighteenth century, unfortunately left us few examples of his
drawings. Apart from his well-known (and overrated) series of portraits on blue
paper, ascribed to his English period, between 1729 and 1739, very few drawings of
other subjects can be attributed to him, but there are some in the Graphische
Sammlung in Munich (Voss, 1918). It is known that Amigoni's early experience
had been in Naples, and there is undoubtedly a certain Giordanesque fluidity to be
seen in his style. Another celebrated Venetian decorative painter, Giambattista
Crosato, had a career that was quite similar to that of Amigoni. Among the best of
the few drawings ascribed to Crosato, apart from those in the Correr, are the ones in
Philadelphia and Providence.

More recent research has brought recognition of other Venetian draughtsmen
active at the start of the eighteenth century. After Grassi, who has been identified as
the author of some sinewy sketches in the British Museum, the Metropolitan, and
in the Bassano Museum (Pignatti, 1984), the greatest artists are Federico
Bencovich and Pittoni. We know little of the former as a draughtsman, and the

21. Giovanni Antonio Pellegrini
(1675-1741)
Adoration of the Magi
Hermitage, Leningrad

22. Giovanni Antonio Guardi (1699-1760)
Aurora
Private collection

drawings of certain attribution in the Correr show his links with seventeenth-century traditions running from Cignani to Celesti, and he only occasionally displays the chiaroscuro liveliness that characterises his dramatic painting (Rizzi, 1982). Many studies by G.B. Pittoni are known, and these illustrate all his styles of drawing, from the initial thought on paper to the *modelletto* or drawing for connoisseurs. Some of these, formerly in the Salvotti collection, were later divided between the Correr, the Galleries and the Cini Foundation in Venice. Stylistically, Pittoni's drawings derive above all from academic methds that are probably based on the drawings of Carracci. He also uses his knowledge of Maratta, gained through his initial training under Balestra, in his sweetness of touch. His finished drawings show the influence of Ricci, of whom he is also basically a follower in painting, using certain sculptural nuances that demonstrate his interest in Piazzetta's style of drawing. Important distinction have recently been made between his drawings and similar ones by Kern, his Hungarian follower (Binion, 1983).

Gaspari Diziani is one of the greatest draughtsmen in eighteenth-century Venice, and he is particularly known for the large collection of his drawings kept in the Correr Museum. Diziani (Fig. 24) is very close to Ricci in his style of painting, but differs substantially from him in drawing, where he seems instead to follow the trend inspired by the open form of Pellegrini and G.A. Guardi. His drawing is characterised by a brilliance that is wholly *rocaille* and he uninterruptedly curls and crumples his line, bringing it back on itself in strong, vigorous, tireless evolutions. It has been possible to reconstruct Diziani's development as a draughtsman through known examples of his drawings that can be linked to datable paintings. He seems to begin in the manner of Ricci, with a style of unbroken outlines and watercolour brushstrokes that produce a sculptural effect; then he sets off towards an increasingly vigorous fragmentation of line, using light in the comparable manner, in a way that has often been confused with the engraving style of Fontebasso. His mature drawings show how fully he adhered to the broad vision of the Venetian Rococo, and are especially reminiscent of Pellegrini, Gian Antonio Guardi, and sometimes the more luminous works of Tiepolo (Dorigato, 1981).

An eclectic style, somewhere between Sebastiano Ricci, Pellegrini and Piepolo, is the common characteristic of much of the drawing of the middle generation. One may enumerate interesting examples by Matteo Bortoloni, A.N. Zannetti, who was famous for his chiaroscuros after Parmigianino and for his caricatures at Windsor and in the Cini Foundatin (Bettagno, 1970), Gerolamo Brusaferro and G.B. Marcuola.

G.B. Piazzetta's drawings have been the subject of much research, and important studies were produced on the occasion of his centenary (Knox, 1983). The real problem is how to distinguish them from the student-exercises from his studio, now known (at least) from the examples of work by Angeli, Cappella, Dall' Oglio, Maggiotto and Giulia Lama, most of which are now kept in the Correr Museum and in the Carrara in Bergamo (Ruggieri, 1973 and 1977). Piazzetta worked in many fields, producing on the one hand anatomical studies and academic drawings from the nude (produced for his school of painting and used by Albrizzi for the prints of his volume of 1760) and on the other drawings for connoisseurs, mostly representing Saints' heads and country people (Fig. 25) in the customary Arcadian manner appreciated at the time. There are examples of these in Windsor, Chicago and Cleveland. Piazzetta uses a technique of charcoal heightened with white chalk, on light-grey or pale-blue paper, which allows brilliant effects of modelling and light. But he also made many drawings for engravers, who illustrated some of the most beautiful books of the time, the best among them being by Pitteri and Cattini. There are large collections of these drawings, almost always in red chalk, in the Albertina, the Hermitage, the Royal Library in Turin and in the Morgan Library. There is also a new and still-growing list of his preparatory drawings in pencil or pen, which were completely unknown until a few years ago (Pignatti, 1973). Several of these have been identified, and these are in the Scholz

23. Giovanni Batista Pittoni (1687-1767)
St Anthony
Museo Correr, Venice

24. Gaspari Diziani (1689-1767)
Judgement of Paris
Museo Correr, Venice

25. Giovanni Batista Piazzetta (1683-1754)
Man in profile
Museo Correr, Venice

collection in New York, and in the National Gallery of Washington. It seems clear that Piazzetta used a taut and architectonic way of drawing when producing this sort of work, a manner which was evidently of Bolognese rather than Venetian inspiration, in which formal structures are indicated by rapid zigzag lines in space.

The work of Giambattista Tiepolo has a prominent place among the drawings of the early eighteenth century. Many important studies have been written on his work as a draughtsman, although the preparation of the corpus of his work is still in progress, which is difficult to complete because of the vast amount of the material, scattered throughout the collections of the world (Knox, 1980). In order to understand the complex subject of Tiepolo's drawings, we must first bear in mind his peculiar method of working, which was carried out in a studio operating as a team with a number of assistants working on the same project, with such a total fusion of style that critics today still find difficulty in distinguishing between the work done by Giambattista and that of his sons, Domenico and Lorenzo, to say nothing of various assistant such as Raggi, Ligari, Menescardi and Zugno.

What is clear is that their frescoes were based on creative sketches by Giambattista, elaborated through an infinite series of working drawings of details (heads, hands, limbs and draperies); sometimes we also have sketches from the

31

26. Giovanni Batista Tiepolo (1696-1770)
Man's head
Scholz collection

hands of various members of the studio (Fig. 26). These are often in black or red
chalk heightened with white, on bluish paper, and were brought together in the past
in several volumes of original sketches, some of which remain in the Correr and the
Hermitage, in addition to the groups of Stuttgart and Würzburg. Originally, there
seemed to be no doubt about attributing of most these black and red chalk drawings
to Giambattista alone, but the problem has since been posed of distinguishing the
work of his sons and his studio assistants. In fact, the method of classifying the
drawings according to the way their themes correspond to the paintings of
Giambattista and Domenico is only partly valid, bearing in mind the peculiar
working methods of the Tiepolos, who also made copies of already-finished works
for the record and as an exercise in drawing. Again, it is sometimes clear that minor
parts painted by Domenico and other assistants can be found in some huge frescoes
largely in the hand of Giambattista, with drawings to correspond. In these cases, we

X Gian Domenico Tiepolo
The Ballad Singers
See no. 37, p. 77

XI Francesco Guardi
The Polignac Wedding Banquet
See no. 99, p. 123

alla nozze del Polignac.

XII Bartolomeo Tarsia
*Triumph of the Olympian
Gods See no. 86, p. 113*

XIII Giuseppe Zais
Landscape with Women Washing
See no. 74, p. 103

XIV Andrea Appiani
Portrait of Eugene de Beauharnais
See no. 109, p. 131

XV Ippolito Caffi
View of Venice
See no. 126, p. 142

XVI Giuseppe Bernardino Bison
Landscape with Fortress and Ferry-Boat
See no. 118, p. 137

Progetto di un Cammino

can conclude that these are genuine preparatory drawings, and not mere copies. Finally, especially in the case of Lorenzo, we can find studies prepared for engraving, which sometimes correspond to his father's drawings.

Where it is possible to make a comparison between original drawings and copies on the same theme, it is clear from his fluid elasticity of line, controlled by the pressure of the hand, that Giambattista's style is the more authoritative and creative. Domenico's line, on the other hand, is thin and hesitant, sometimes shaky, often traced over: in addition, the thickness of the line never changes, as if he were using a reed-pen and not the charcoal or soft red chalk of his father's drawings. Lorenzo's style is more elementary, mainly relying on hatched shading, and he appears to be mostly a copyist, whose inclination was towards the style of engraving (Pignatti, 1974).

The attribution of their pen-drawings, many of which were originally produced for collectors, is much easier, and there is in fact no difficulty in distinguishing between them, so evident is the power of Giambattista's style. An enormous

27. Giovanni Batista Tiepolo (1696-1770)
Anthony and Cleopatra
Metropolitan Museum of Art, New York

number of collections of these drawings are preserved in European collections, in the Horne, the Victoria and Albert, the museums of Stuttgart, Würzburg, Leningrad and Trieste, in addition to the American collections in the Morgan Library, the Metropolitan and Fogg Museums and the Heinemann collection in New York.

One question remains about these pen-drawings, and this concerns the caricatures, where it is not difficult, however, to work out a way of distinguishing between them, if we move backwards from the scenes featuring Punchinello and the drawings signed by Domenico. Giambattista's caricatures are often sketchly, but they are recognisable by their flexible and varied line, which has an entirely chromatic quality, and by their fluid and architectonic manner, set in his usual dazzling luminosity. These caricatures are to be found in the Correr, Lehman, Princeton University and Metropolitan Museum collections (Fig. 27).

Among Tiepolo's successors and followers, Francesco Fontebasso unquestionably deserves a chapter to himself in the history of eighteenth-century Venetian art, for his qualities as a draughtsman and an engraver. In his many finished drawings, among them those in the Correr and in Princeton, Fontebasso achieves an individual style which is closer to Ricci and Tiepolo than to the open manner of Pellegrini and Gian Antonio Guardi (Byam Shaw, 1954; Pignatti, 1981).

As for other well-known decorative painters, active primarily in fresco painting, until a few years ago, we lacked enough of their drawings to make reliable attributions. Recent research has allowed us to track down some drawings by Francesco Zugno, Jacopo Marieschi and Jacopo Guarana. They can be placed midway between Ricci and Tiepolo, and their style seems to be inspired by both of them. Zugno seems to be the most remarkable of these artists. There is a particular detailed incisiveness which is rarely seen in his frescoes, but which can be found especially in the delicate chiaroscuro sketches which are often related to them, and which are now in the Correr Museum, the Philadelphia Museum and the Manning collection.

The earliest eighteenth-century Venetian landscape painter we shall consider is Marco Ricci, who was the nephew of Sebastiano, and an engraver and draughtsman (Pilo, 1963; Martini, 1982.) In general, his sketches are not unlike his actual paintings; this is the case especially with his gouaches and his temperas on kidskin. A Ricci landscape always exhales a special classical aura, and the clear-cut treatement and diaphanous luminosity of his watercolours or his typical golden-brown ink recall the effects of drawings by Titian and Domenico Campagnola (Fig. 28). Ricci most probably turned to the work of Salvator Rosa to perfect this

28. Marco Ricci (1676-1730)
The Assault
Scholz collection

29. Giovanni Battista Piranesi (1720-1778)
Capriccio
Ashmolean Museum, Oxford

inspiration: he had become acquainted with it during his early journeys to Rome and Naples. It is also possible, from the luminous clarity of his results, that he was inspired by the work of Poussin. There are many drawings by Ricci in Windsor and in American collections, especially those of Cleveland, Princeton, Providence and the Scholz collection.

Other characteristics of Ricci's discovery of Salvator Rosa is the introduction to the Venetian circle of the apparatus of ruin-painting, typical of the Roman-Neapolitan tradition, and of a mottling effect that inspired the painters of battle-scenes who followed Callot and Borgognone.

Giambattista Piranesi's drawings were indebted in his early days to Ricci's inspiration as a landscapist, together with the influence of Tiepolo and Canaletto. We mention him only briefly, since he was soon absorbed by the Roman circle, though he never forgot his Venetian artistic training. There are examples of his work in Hamburg, the British Museum, in Berlin, the Uffizi and the Morgan Library (Bettagno, 1978; Robinson, 1978; Fig. 29).

The painters of battle-scenes also make marked references to Ricci: one has only to look at the drawings of Francesco Simonini, whose work begins in this specialized tradition, as he was a pupil of Monti, who imitated Borgognone: there is a fine series of these drawings in the Correr. Simonini is traditionally regarded as the teacher of Giuseppe Zais, and this is already confirmed by many examples of his work in the same genre of battle-painting. Above all, though, Zais was a landscape painter in the manner of Marco Ricci, and this can be seen especially in his pen and watercolour drawings, and in his coloured tempera studies on paper in the Correr

30. Francesco Zuccarelli (1702-88)
Rustic landscape
Windsor Castle
Reproduced by gracious permission of Her Majesty the Queen

Museum and the Metropolitan. Francesco Zuccarelli's work is superior in quality: he was a little older than Zais, and is remarkable for his sketches in red chalk or pencil, and for his pen-drawings, which he often finished for connoisseurs with shading in sepia and watercolour, or lightly touched up with tempera or white (Bassi-Rathgeb, 1948). These drawings are in the Uffizi, the Correr, and the museums of Chicago and Detroit (Fig. 30), Providence and the Scholz collection.

Thanks to the interest shown in them by collectors, the drawings of the view-painters, beginning with one of the founders of the genre, Luca Carlevaris, are very well-known. The work of Carlevaris is to be found almost entirely in Europe, in the sketchbooks held in the Correr and in the British Museum. His style achieves remarkable effects, especially in the sensitive recording of appearances in his small figures, which he drew from the life (Rizzi, 1967).

The work of Antonio Canal (Canaletto) is of a much higher poetic value (Fig. 31), for he was one of the universal geniuses of graphic art, and was capable of creating exceptional drawings and engraving (Constable–Links, 1976). For Canaletto drawing could be of two distinct types: instrumental drawing, for the study and preparation of views, and finished drawing for sale to connoisseurs. Documentary drawings, such as those for the *Quaderno delle Gallerie* in Venice were among the former, and there are others in the Fogg Museum of Cambridge, Mass., and in the Philadelphia Museum. Canaletto clearly used these sketches, and probably other even more summary ones, drawn from the life by means of the portable camera, *obscura* to construct his views of Venice (Pignatti, 1958 and 1969). Canaletto's most important block of finished drawings, together with the group in the British Museum, is in Windsor, bought directly by the English diplomat and merchant-amateur Joseph Smith, who was in Venice from about 1700 to 1770. A number of these drawings are also preserved in America, in almost every museum and in the major private collections, in Boston, Chicago, Cleveland, Philadelphia, the National Gallery and the Lehman and Scholz collections.

Although his manner changes across the span of his activities, one constant feature of Canaletto's drawings is an extraordinary synthesis of line and light, which is often expressed in impressionistic shorthand marks, instantaneous in their effect.

The drawings of Canaletto's nephew Bernardo Bellotto are often more realistic; he often approaches Canaletto's style in his pen-drawings of views of cities, like those in the Darmstadt Museum, but he is identifiable by a sharper line that is typical of his later career as a precise and detailed engraver, in his long period of work in Dresden and Warsaw (Kozakiewicz, 1972).

31. Antonio Canaletto (1697-1768)
Piazzetta
Windsor Castle
Reproduced by gracious permission of Her Majesty the Queen

32. Pietro Longhi (1702-85)
Venetian Senator
Lehman collection

The work of Pietro Longhi is unique in the history of eighteenth-century Venetian drawing (Fig. 32). Most of his drawings are kept in the Correr Museum, and there are also some beautiful examples in Berlin, and in the Morgan Library. They are almost unchanging in their technique of pencil or black chalk heightened with white on yellowish or grey paper, and most of them are preparatory sketches for the little paintings that made Longhi's reputation: he was more a portraitist of social classes, modes and customs than of individuals. Their exceptional quality is their faithful derivation from life, evidenced by the many written notes pointing out the colours to be used. The most astonishing thing is the total detachment of Pietro Longhi's style of drawing from that of all contemporary Venetian examples. The closest counterparts to these drawings can be found, if anywhere, in the work of his French comtemporaries, from Watteau to Lancret, and perhaps even more in certain drawings by Chardin (Pignatti, 1968).

Giandomenico Tiepolo holds an important position in the field of genre-painting. Apart from his collaborative work in his family's pictorial enterprises, he devoted himself to independent production of paintings and drawings, especially after his father's death (Fig. 33). His drawings show a particular talent for humour, with a marked tendency towards scenes of a social character, though these lack the genuine political spirit shown by Hogarth or most of all by Goya in an analogous epoch (Mariuz, 1971). Most of the famous series of *Pulcinella* sketches or the caricature scenes are in America, in Boston, Cleveland, the Metropolitan Museum and in San Francisco.

The last generation of the great century of the Rococo had meanwhile vanished along with Domenico Tiepolo. Amongst them was Pier Antonio Novelli, who was more remarkable as a draughtsman than as a painter, and whose style is characterised by a line as thin and fluent as an engraver's; there is a fine collection of his work in the Correr and in the Cooper Hewitt Museum. Others were the professional engravers, Francesco Bartolozzi and Antonio Zucchi, who brought the art of eighteenth-century Venetian drawing to a conclusion. We have now entered the age of Antonio Canova, a sculptor who was also remarkable for his

33. Domenico Tiepolo (1727-1804)
At the Market
Private collection

34. Francesco Guardi (1712-93)
The Bucintoro on Ascension Day
Prince's Gate collection

delicate figure-drawings inspired by the late eighteenth-century Venetian milieu. Bernardo Bisson is one of the last voices in the great tradition: he was endowed with an eclectic style of drawing, imitated from Guardi, Canaletto, Tiepolo and Novelli, and recent studies have reassessed his work. His drawings are in the Correr, in the Osio collection in Milan, and in the Boston, Cleveland, Providence and Metropolitan Museums (Rizzi, 1976).

Francesco Guardi left an impressive number of drawings of all types and qualities in the Correr and in the Louvre. In American collections, the most important group is in the Metropolitan, followed by those in the Fogg Museum and in Cleveland (Morassi, 1975). We already have partial catalogues to the most remarkable of these collections (Pallucchini, 1943; Pignatti, 1983).

Guardi's manner of drawing is characterized by an absolutely unique rapidity of touch, owing its inspiration to a wide range of artistic influences from the caricatures of Callot to the tormented figures of Magnasco (Fig. 34). After this early period, in which he was still partly indebted to his first master, his brother Gian Antonio, Francesco Guardi devoted himself entirely to views of Venice, where his work became a sort of alternative to Canaletto's production. Francesco Guardi's imagery is set within the framework of a complete recollection of the luminous atmosphere of Venice, seen as a fragmentary space which invites the most unexpected experiments, and represented in a way that is typical of the light and airy uncertainty of eighteenth-century Rococo. Guardi links himself in this way to the tradition of the view-painters, but transcends their originally documentary and illuministic spirit, and seems to go beyond the decorative manner of representation characteristic of his time, and to open the way towards the Romantic vision.

Francesco Guardi's elevated poetic quality also becomes evident if one compares his work with the imitations made over a long period by his son Giacomo, the major collection of which is in the Correr (Dorigato, 1983). We now enter the modern age, and with these minor works, often destined for the tourist trade, the glorious course of Venetian drawing comes to an end.

Catalogue of Works

List of artists

Ercole de Roberti (c. 1450-1496)
I. *Battle Scene*
Inv. no. 21.
Black pencil, pen and brush and black ink on vellum; 195 x 290 mm.
Prov.: Correr, 1830. *Lit:* Vienna Pub., 1909, n. 812; Longhi, 1934, p. 139; Gronore, 1934, p. 27; Ortolani, 1941, p. 163; Popham–Pouncey, 1950, p. 114; Ruberna, 1962, p. 246; De Nicolò Salmazo, 1980, figs. 37 and 45.

Given to Parentino in 1909, but Longhi (1934) attributed the conception of this remarkable drawing to Ercole de Roberti, while he thought that the execution was not by the artist. Ortolani, on the other hand, gave the drawing completely to Ercole (op. cit.). In fact, this sheet presents some stylistic characters, such as the metallic and elongated forms and the nervous movement sweeping across the scene, which can be related to the Ferrarese school, but at the same time it is clearly reminiscent of Mantegna's expressive style. It has been suggested, therefore, also an attribution to the workshop of the Istrian painter Bernando Parentino, if not to the artist himself, who can be considered one of the most important artists active in Padua after Mantegna. He is documented to have worked there, in the years 1492-96, at the frescoes decorating the arches of the main cloister of the monastery of S. Giustina and depicting episodes from the life of St. Benedict (De Nicolò Salmazo, op. cit., 1980).

Parentino's paintings and drawings show an archaeological taste which is typically Mantegnesque, but at the same time an extremely personal and intense expressiveness and linear tension.

This battle scene could perhaps have connections with two fragments of the same subject appearing on the cloister of S. Giustina. One battle scene is painted as a fragment in the *Leaving of St Benedict from Norcia* (op. cit., p. 106, fig. 37) and the other is inserted in the episode of the *Calling and Taking the Habit of St. Benedict*, painted on the sixth arch of the cloister (op. cit., p. 118, fig. 45).

The nude-types and the helmets appearing in the present sheet are very similar to those of the *Roman Triumph* in the British Museum (Popham–Pouncey, 1950, p. 114), the drawing of which has also been attributed to Parentino. In both the London and Correr sheets the precise and incisive outlines and the evenly regulated parallel hatching applied to build up the internal modelling are reminiscent of Montagna's style.

However, most recent research, conducted by Joseph Manca at Columbia University, has pointed out that the former attribution to de Roberti should be taken again as valid. In fact, that painter made many battle scenes in some of his paintings, such as the Cini *Madonna*, the *Pala portuense* and the *Dormition of the Virgin*. The style of the drawing is representative of a style which tends to evoke the antique: and for this reason there shows connections with the Paduan school. The possible proposed date is when Roberti was court painter in Ferrara in the 1490s.

Albrecht Durer (1471-1528)
2. *St. Anne*
Inv. no.: 8222.
Brush and sepia wash, heightened with white; grey paper on support sheet; 399 x 287 mm.
Inscr.: 'A.D. 1522' (in the artist's hand); 'Alberto Durer' (in an eighteenth-century hand); on the verso: 'Agnes in schwartz' (in a sixteenth-century hand).
Prov.: Correr, 1830. *Lit.:* Winkler, 1939, no. 853; Panofsky, 1948, no. 767; Van Gelder, 1971, 158, fig. 2; Strieder, 1971, no. 226; Pignatti, 1980, no. 432.
Exhibitions: Nuremberg, 1971, no. 226; Paris, 1978.

This large drawing by Dürer (formerly in the volume of prints B 23 no. 208) belongs to a group of half-length figures which can be dated around 1520, yet being characterized by the brush-technique 'grey on grey'. Winkler (1939, no. 853) saw it close to the Albertina St. Anne (ibid., no. 574) of 1519, identifying in this sheet another probable portrait of Agnes Dürer, the painter's wife (the contemporary inscription deciphered by Winkler accordingly says 'Agnes in schwartz').

According to Van Gelder (1971, 158), it would be a re-elaboration of the portrait of Dürer's sister Metzgen in the Custodia Foundation in Paris. Panofsky's suggestion seems rather more acceptable (1948, no. 767) that this drawing is a half-length study for one of the Saints of the Sacra Conversazione planned by Dürer in 1521-22, drawings of which are at the Louvre and at Bayonne (Panofsky, 1948, nos. 762-765).

Bonifazio De'Pitati (1487-1553)
3. *Holy Family*
Inv. no.: 1719.
Pen and sepia; 70 x 68 mm.
Prov.: Gamba, 1841. *Lit.:* Pignatti, 1980,
no. 45.

The traditional characterization of Bonifazio as the 'anti-Titian', substantially
accepted by Westphal (1931) and Tietze
(1944), made the attribution of his drawings
even more difficult. Really a few of those
catalogued by the Tietzes can certainly be
ascribed to him, mostly in his later activity,
when the Veronese artist shows some
contacts with his best pupil, Schiavone.

Besides, in our opinion, the definition of
Bonifazio's early activity is still open, even
because the influence of Titian – either
accepted or rejected – is undeniable, as one
can clearly see from his paintings. None of
the drawings that the critics have proposed
until now appears to belong to his early
period, which, even though 'ab absurdo',
should be defined as Titianesque. And it is to
this period that this drawing of the Holy
Family seems to belong, with its arrow-like
hatching, reminiscent of a xylography,
which recalls Titian's drawings around
1510-20. Also the iconographic comparison
with the paintings leads to the attribution to
Bonifazio: the group of the Holy Family, as a
matter of fact, is very close to that of the
Hermitage, while the round-shaped
Madonna, the plump child, and the elderly
St. Joseph reappear in the formerly
Campbell paingting in Glasgow (repr. in
Westphal, 1931, figs. 7 and 37).

Carletto Caliari (1570-1596)
4. *Two Peasant Girls*
Inv. no.: 1704
Red pencil, yellowish paper; 185 x 120 mm.
Inscr.: "da Titian" (Gamba?-sec. XIX)
Prov.: Gamba, 1841.
Lit.: unpublished.

The fine quality of this drawing, and its charming composition of peasant girls against a background of landscape with woods, hills, houses and a bridge, make it worthy of attention even if attribution is difficult. The inscription 'da Tiziano' is little use, as it was clearly made in the nineteenth century, when the drawing received an ink rule as a surround, a device signifying that the drawing was in Gamba's collection, as on other drawings from him in the Correr.

Pictorially, the handling of the landscape is close to some of the realistic views in Maser's frescoes, so the drawing could have come from his circle, though it is not from his hand. Some of the elements in the drawing do point significantly towards a possible attribution to his followers. In particular, there is the influence of Montemazzano, whose *Portrait of a Lady*, in Darmstadt (T. 906), recalls in its pose and coiffure (though more elaborate) the figures in this drawing. Closer still in typology and style is the drawing from Maser's circle, of a woman's head, inscribed as being of Giulia Palma, the wife of Antonio, now in Erlagen (T. 820), in which the background, reminiscent of Bonifacio, is the point of contact with this drawing. This brings us to the *Portrait of Andriana Palma* in the Morgan Library, a known drawing by Carletto, dated 1591, and suggests an attribution to the same artist. This would also account for the influence of Bassano's late work, for example in the long vertical lines of the pleating in the girls' dresses, which we find in drawings by Lenado, such as the *Leander* in the British Museum (T. 222). Also, if this choice restricts us to Maser's more 'classical' followers, this explains the inclusion of two children in the background, not altogether consistent with a peasant subject. The balanced and slightly academic approach to the composition recalls the style of Haeredes Paoli, some of whose drawings, for example in Windsor, could still be attributed to Carletto.

Jacopo Bassano (c. 1515-1592)
5. *Adoration of the Shepherds*
Inv. no. 1402.
Red chalk; 196 x 290 mm.
Inscr.: '20', 'J. Bassano' (pen, in a nineteenth-century hand); '914' (pencil, in a nineteenth-century hand).
Prov.: Zoppetti, 1852. *Lit:* Pignatti, 1980, no. 22.
Verso: Adoration of the Shepherds
Red chalk.
Inscr.: Cl. III, 1402 (red pencil, in a nineteenth-century hand).
This important sheet can be ascribed to Jacopo Bassano for its high quality and its many correspondences with his paintings and drawings. The subject of the *Adoration of the Shepherds* is related, on the recto, to the painting *Giusti del Giardino* and the one in Hampton Court (repr. in Arslan, 1960, figs. 71 and 74); on the verso the same subject appears in the painting by Gerolamo da Ponte in Vienna (repr. in Arslan, 1960, fig. 340), as a proof that the sheet was circulating in the circle of the Bassanesque workshop. The broad, arrow-like lines, clotted in the typical spheric heads, are identical to those of other creative drawings by Jacopo, as the famous sheet in Ottawa depicting the *Presentation*, dated 1569 (repr. in Tietze, 1944, no. 177); the same characteristics, also for the architectural elements, can be found in Albertina *Solomon* (repr. in Stix-Froelich-Brun, 1926, no. 74). Therefore, this sheet should be dated around 1565-70, in strict connection with the execution of paintings whose subject-matter is very common in the Bassanesque artistic production.

Sante Peranda (1566-1638)
7. *Virgin and Child with Three Saints*
Inv. no. 1060.
Pen and sepia wash; 220 x 160 mm.
Inscr.: 'Peranda'.
Prov.: Correr, 1830. *Lit.:* unpublished.
Not much is known about this Venetian painter who was a pupil and collaborator of Palma il Giovane. His activity was dedicated mainly to religious painting and this sketch is probably a compositional study for an altar-piece. There is a chalk drawing in the Uffizi, showing a Virgin and Child, half length, and bearing an old inscription: 'Sante Peranda' (Tietze and Tietze–Courat, 1944, no. 1274, pl. CLXXXIV). The Virgin and Child's pose is very similar to that of the present sheet.

Jacopo Palma il Giovane (1544-1628)
6. *Christ Standing in a Chalice Supported by Angels*
Inv. no. 1242.
Pen and brown ink; 268 x 191 mm.
Inscr.: n 61 Palma.
Prov.: Correr. *Lit.:* Tietze–Courat, 1944, p. 222, no. 1179; Andrews, 1968, p. 84, no. D 3099, fig. 590.
As the Tietzes have pointed out, a similar drawing is in the National Gallery of Scotland, Edinburgh (Andrews, 1968, fig. 590). According to them, the composition resembles the frontispiece of the Mariegola of the brotherhood of the Scuola del Santissimo Corpo di Cristo, in S. Agnese in Venice. This page, which is in the Correr Museum (Ms. IV, 25), contains a miniature showing the same arrangement except that the angels carry the instruments of the passion of Christ. Andrews, in his catalogue of the National Gallery of Scotland drawings, states that the Tietzes's observation, although correct, is of less significance than may at first appear, as the subject seems to have occured rather frequently in the popular art of the period and similar images were used in church services. It is an allegorical representation of the Eucharistic sacrifice and the present drawing was probably a preparatory sketch for the decoration of a tabernacle shutter. The same subject is quite often found also in Palma il Giovane's paintings.

The style would suggest that this is a late drawing, executed around 1620.

Pevanda

SIXTEENTH CENTURY

Aliense (Antonio Vassilacchi called) (1556-1629)
8. *River Gods*
Inv. no. 8294
Red chalk, pen and sepia; white paper on support sheet; 130 x 207 mm.
Prov.: Musatti, 1967. *Lit.:* Pignatti, 1970-71, no. 7; Idem, 1980, no. 1.
Exhibitions: Venice, 1970, no. 7.
Ridolfi (II, 1924, pp. 207-222) stresses Aliense's particular devotion to drawing; however, his catalogue by Tietze and Tietze–Courat (1944), who wrote the artist's best biography published until now, does not reach 20 numbers. Absolutely certain drawings are missing, among which the most probable example is the *Annunciation* in Oxford (Tietze–Courat, no. 14), whose verso bears the attribution to the Aliense in Ridolfi's hand. Besides, the Tietzes recognized in the *Two Struggling Men* in the Rasini collection (no. 12) the preparatory drawing for the *Victory of Carlo Zeno over the*

Genoese in the Ducal Palace, painting which can be dated from the years 1578-85. The drawing demonstrates the Aliense's graphic style in the moment of transition from his first Veronese training to the subsequent influence of Tintoretto, interpreted, however, with great attention to the flickering line of Palma il Giovane.

The sheet with *Three River Gods*, arrived at the Correr with the Musatti collection, could easily be related to the Aliense's style, particularly in his early period, still reminiscent of Veronese's fluid lights and light-effects. The volumetric plasticity of the nudes is reminiscent of the Rasini drawing, with which this sheet is thought to be contemporary.

Andrea de' Michieli called Il Vicentino (1542-1617)
9. Apollo Enchanting the Animals
Inv. no. 1742.
Pen and brown ink and sepia wash; yellowish paper on support sheet; 164 x 214 mm (oval).
Inscr.: 'Arpin' (in an eighteenth-century hand)
Prov.: Gamba, 1841. *Lit.:* unpublished.
We had originally attributed this drawing to the painter Ludovico Dorigny, noting some stylistic similarities with another drawing by the same artist in the Castelvecchio Museum, Verona, which shows the Taurus and the Gemini, and is a study for the fresco decoration of the Villa Allegri (now Arvedi) of Cuzzano Veronese (Bettagno, 1963, no. 25). However, we would suggest now an attribution to Andrea Vicentino, who was Vicentine by origin and is not mentioned in Venice before 1583 (book of the painter's guild).

This drawing presents the same coloristic effects and late Mannerist character of another ascribed to Vicentino by the Tietzes (1944, no. 2229, pl. CXXXIX), which shows the Flaying of Marsyas and it is in the Ashmolean Museum, Oxford. The Tietzes date it from around the end of the sixteenth century and we would suggest a similar date also for the present drawing.

Luca Cambiaso (1527-1585)
10. Sibyl with Putto
Inv. no. 1748.
Black pencil, pen and sepia wash; white paper on support sheet; 318 x 215 mm.
Inscr.: 'Luca Giordano' (in an eighteenth-century hand).
Prov.: Gamba, 1841. *Lit.:* Pignatti, 1980, no. 55.
In Cambiaso's extensive graphic production, the 'cubic' drawings, as this one depicting a Sibyl, belong to every period of his activity. Here, however, the rather stiff and broken lines seem to indicate a quite late period, and certainly – one might say – later than the

Venetian experiences in which the artist came into contact with the silvery luminosity of Veronese's canvases.

While the iconography is referred to pictures like the *Liberal Arts* in a Milanese collection (repr. in Suida-Manning, 1958, figs. 59-62), the graphic style recalls his later drawings, probably of the years 1570-75, as *Venus and Adonis* at Chatsworth (repr. in Suida-Manning, 1958, fig. 342). A figure seen from behind in the *Ascent to Calvary* in a Genoese private collection, published by Torriti (1969, plate XXX), shows a very similar anatomical treatment and the same 'cubic' hatching.

55

SIXTEENTH CENTURY

Vincenzo Scamozzi (1552-1616)
11. *Design for a Tomb*
Inven. no. 6097.
Pen and wash, sepia.
Front and side elevation: various measurements and notes.
Prov.: Wcowich-Lazzari, 1896. *Lit.:* Scolari, 1837, p. 147; Selvatico Lazzari, 1852, p. 120; Puppi-Olivato Puppi, 1974, pp. 54-80.

This drawing by Vincenzo Scamozzi has been connected since the nineteenth century with the funerary monument to the Dolfin family in the church of San Salvador (Scolari). It shows a close resemblance to the monument, but recently some significant and authoritative 'disquieting differences' have been brought to light (Puppi-Puppi Olivato). Although the shading of the architectural framework of the *depositorio* (in the context of an already-existing brick wall of identical articulation) argues consistently in favour of recognising this as a drawing of the Dolfin monument in question, there is a discrepancy in the dates of the execution of the monument itself, according to Timofiewitsch, who ascribes it entirely to Campagna. One could then agree (with the Puppis) that this was an initial design by Scamozzi, ordered by Andrea Dolfin for his wife Benedetta, later modified and executed by Campagna after 1602, the year of Andrea Dolfin's death. In that case it is not hard to recognise the central bust in this drawing as that of a woman, as are the two statues on their high pedestals, while the *scenette* in low relief could be interpreted as a weddingscene – but we are wandering into a treacherous area of delicate conjecture.

At any rate, it is a work of highly significant quality as a drawing, as well as being of architectural importance within Scamozzi's corpus of work. The result of his selfconfident treatment of the sculptural decoration, taken as a whole, is very effective, while the illustrative technique in the design of the architectural elements is skilfully achieved.

Marcantonio Bassetti (1586-1630)
12. *Study for a Boxer*
Inv. no. 1147.
Black pencil and sepia wash, heightened with white; bluish paper on support sheet; 410 x 231 mm.
Inscr.: 'Marc'Antonio Bassetti' (in a seventeenth-century hand).
Prov.: Correr, 1830. *Lit.:* Pignatti, 1980, no. 30.
This beautiful drawing can be technically related to other well-known drawings by Bassetti, and its attribution is further confirmed by the contemporary inscription, which appears to be true. The plastic modelling of the anatomy recalls drawings like the *Entombment of Christ* in Windsor, no. 4833- cat. 1619, (repr. in Blunt–Croft-Murray, 1957, fig. 8); the right-turning torso can be connected with the models of the Agostiniani altarpiece in the Schleissheim Museum (repr. in Magagnato, 1974, fig. 148).

Niccolo' Renieri (1590-1677)
13. *Roman Charity*
Inv. no. 5744.
Red chalk; yellowish paper. 177 x 167 mm.
Inscr.: 'Cavagliere Ranieri' (in the artist's
hand); 'Nicolò Renieri' (in a sixteenth-
century hand).
Prov.: Molin, 1813. *Lit.:* Muraro, 1953, 20;
Pignatti, 1954, 310; Idem, 1959, 46.

This is Renieri's only certain drawing. It
already belongs to the artist's Venetian
period, that is to say after 1625. The typical
shot-like effects of Renieri's luminous paintings are marked by the elongated, loose and
articulated-in-space lines. Several paintings,
such as the *Female Figures* in the Accademia
Galleries or the Correr Museum, confirm
the sheet's attribution to Renieri. The

classical trend is clear, in connection with the
Carraccesque style which Renieri followed
in his early period, when he was moving
between Rome and Venice.

Bernardo Strozzi (1581-1644)
14. *Study of a Male Head*
Inv. no. 1626.
Black chalk on carboard; 256 x 217 mm.
Lit.: Pignatti, 1981, 204.
This charming drawing by Bernardo Strozzi
could be dated from his last Genoese or his
first Venetian period, that is around 1630-35.
The handling is softer in comparison with his
earlier work. The head has some similarities
with Strozzi's *Lute Player* in the Kunsthistorisches Museum, Vienna (Mortari,
1966, p. 189, fig. 417).

Francesco Maffei (1606-1660)
15. *Man in Armour*
Inv. no. 1416.
Black chalk and grey wash; 350 x 270 mm.
Inscr.: 'Van Dyck'.
Lit.: unpublished.
This drawing was given to Daniel Van Dyck
in the old inventories. We suggest an attribution to Francesco Maffei, born in Vicenza
and a pupil of Maganza. In the Museum of
Bassano there is a study for a martyr's head
ascribed to Maffei (Magagnato, 1956), which
shows a similar handling. Typically Baroque
are the light effects and an almost sensual
feeling for texture noticeable in the treatment of the armour. No painting by Maffei is
known, which can be closely related to this
drawing, probably a study for a portrait.

Johan Carl Loth (1632-1698)
16. *St. Mark*
Inv. no. 975
Pen and sepia wash; 177 x 158 mm
Prov.: Correr, 1830. *Lit.:* unpublished.
This drawing seems to belong to Loth's first
Venetian period, shortly after 1655. The
head of the old Evangelist is in fact quite
close to that of the shepherd carrying a jug
behind Mercury in the painting entitled
*Philemon and Baucis giving hospitality to
Jupiter and Mercury* in the Kunsthistorisches
Museum, Vienna (Ewald, 1965, no. 411),
and that of Argus in *Mercury and Argus* in the
National Gallery, London, (Ewald, 1965,
no. 422). Both the paintings belong to the
artist's first Venetian period.

SEVENTEENTH CENTURY

Antonio Zanchi (1631-1722)
17. *The Finding of Moses*
Inv. no. 5408.
Pencil, pen and red wash on yellowish paper;
430 x 300 mm.
Prov.: Molin, 1813. *Lit.:* Riccoboni, 1967;
Pignatti, 1981.
There are only a few drawings which can be
certainly ascribed to Antonio Zanchi, also
because his graphic style changes a lot during
his very long activity.

The present drawing seems to be a rapid
compositional sketch, to fix down on paper
the first idea, probably for a painting.
However no painting by Zanchi related to
this drawing is known. The broad brush
strokes and the more or less transparent
washes which creates the chiaroscuro are
reminiscent of Celesti's manner, such as that
of the *Expulsion of Heliodorus*, also in the
Correr Museum (Pignatti, 1981, p. 201,
fig. 5).

Andrea Celesti (1637-1706)
18. *Solomon and The Queen of Sheba*
Inv. no. 1856.
Pen and sepia; Havana brown paper on
supporting cardboard; 147 x 475 mm.
Inscr.: 'Celesti pinxit' (in an eighteenth-
century hand).
Prov.: Zoppetti, 1852. *Lit.:* Pignatti, 1980,
no. 207; Idem, 1981.
The study of Celesti's graphic production
has taken little steps, and only in recent
times. The first drawing which has been
attributed to him with some certainty is the
Expulsion of Heliodorus in the Correr,
no. 5409, for its undoubted correspondence
with the artist's late pictorial style, when he
was moving between Brescia and Toscolano,
and the iconographic relationship with some
of those pictures (Pignatti, 1954, 313).
Morassi then pointed out the *David with
Goliath's Head*, exhibited at the Mostra del
Seicento a Venezia, and also datable around
the 1690s for the reference to the painting in
Casa Parisini at Gargnano (Pignatti, 1959,
no. 83). To these were then added the
Allegory for the Loggia of Brescia, c. 1700, now
in the Metropolitan (repr. in Bean-Stampfle,
1967, no. 129) and the *Probatica Piscina* in the
Art Institute, Chicago, signed, and related by
us to the painting formerly in the Church of
the Ascension near Piazza S. Marco, which
was demolished at the beginning of the
nineteenth century (Pignatti, 1974, no. 45).

Celesti's graphic style is characterized by
a picturesque looseness of touch; the dynamic
lines tend to stress the pictorial effects which
are so characteristic of this artist, who played
an essential role in the formation of the
Venetian Rococo pictorial language.
Considering all this, it seems logical to
include in Celesti's small catalogue this new
sheet showing *Solomon and the Queen of
Sheba*, which corresponds completely to the
stylistic characteristics above mentioned.
From the iconographic point of view, the

drawing might be the first idea for the
painting of the same subject in the Bettoni
Cazzago palace in Brescia (repr. in Mucchi-
Della Croce, 1954, fig. 33). However, here
the conception is more scenographic, and it
rather recalls, in the projection of the foreground against the background colonnade
opening onto a brightly lit area, the setting of
David and Goliath, and even better, of the
Probatica Piscina in Chicago. A painting
depicting *Tamerlanie and Bajazet*, in the
Neues Palais in Potsdam, probably executed
by Celesti in the 1690s, (repr. in Mucchi-
Della Croce, 1954, fig. 29), shows a composition stretching horizontally, with many
elements in common with this drawing
(there is a print of it by Cunego, executed in
1788). It must be considered in the end that
the sheet bears a valid eighteenth-century
inscription 'Celesti pinxit'; the squaring
indicates that the drawing was used as a
modello for the execution of a very large
canvas (a good 22·feet! (6.7 m)).

Antonio Gaspari (c. 1660 – between 1738 and 1749)

19. *Design for the High Altar in S. Moise*
Inv. no. 6986, I, 11.
Pen and wash, sepia; 822 (max) x 396 mm.
Inscr.: below left within a coat of arms: 'Antonius Gaspari Venetus Inv.'; *verso*, pen, 'Altar Maggior nella Chiesa di S. Moise (aut.)
Prov.: Davis & Orioli 1935. *Lit.:* Bassi 1962 and 1963 no. 10.

This drawing shows one of Antonio Gaspari's most astonishing architectural and sculptural inventions. The project was prepared as a commission from the rebuilders of the Church of S. Moise for an apsidal chapel and high altar, but was only completed (according to Bassi's careful reconstruction, 1963, pp. 58, 62) in a reduced version by Alessandro Tremignon. The altar of S. Moise is a typically theatrical Baroque construction,

and shows a uniquely melodramatic and narrative formulation, unfolding the story of Moses on Mount Sinai in scenes that follow one another. The game that Gaspari plays develops entirely through a sense of a careful counterposition between varied and contrasting elements: the casual naturalness of the masses and clouds in the upper section and the orderly geometrical division into compartments of the altar itself; the airy transparency of the effects of light and the weight of the stone (brought by the sculptor Meyring in the complete altar to an incredible and unnatural mirror-like polish, underlining the further element of alienating contrast between the material and what it imitates); the precise and classical spatiality of the great arch and the overwhelming, explosive cascade of indefinite shapes, and so on.

Soon after the troubled transfer of author-

ity from Gaspari to Tremignon, this drawing was engraved with a dedication to Bernardo Nave in 1685, together with other drawings, also by Gaspari, for the same altar.

Antonio Gaspari

20. *Design for the Tomb of Francesco Morosini, 'Il Peloponnesiaco' in S. Stefano*
Inv. no. 6986, I, 59.
Pen and wash, sepia, watercolour retouched in Indian ink. 482 x 350 mm.
Prov.: Davis & Orioli, 1935. *Lit.:* Bassi, 1962 and 1963.

This drawing is probably the definitive version of the series of ideas that Gaspari submitted for the tomb in the Church of S. Stefano ordered by Doge Francesco Morosini in a codicil to his will drawn up in 1693.

Gaspari left other analogous drawings in preparation for this scheme, though these were based on Bernini's earlier design of 1669 for the Duke of Beaufort's catafalque in the church of Aracoeli in Rome, preserved in a drawing by Bernini (in London) and in a print by De Rossi (Bassi, 1963, pp. 68-69).

The bust of the Doge is the one Filippo Parodi sculpted for the Doge's Palace, while the scenes in the various sections of the pyramid-obelisk depict Morosini's exploits in battle.

The outline of the cenotaph, with its curved central section and lateral wings with jutting corners, is unique in Venice: it was 'copied literally', according to Bassi, from Bernini's catafalque for Beaufort, and Gaspari put it forward again in the catafalque that he in his turn built for the funeral of Morosini, who died at Napoli di Romania in 1694.

Amongst the vast amount of work that Gaspari produced for the Morosini family (including his fascinating proposals for the façade of the Church of S. Vidal, designed to commemorate *Il Peloponnesiaco*), the project shown in our drawing has a lively formulation and a uniquely successful scenographic effect. Even the choice of polychrome marbles, clearly indicated in the water-colour drawing, emphasizes all the florid, delirious exuberance that is the decorative and imaginative trademark of Antonio Gaspari's Baroque style.

Andrea Tirali (1657-1737)
21. *The Valier Tomb in SS. Giovanni e Paolo*
Inv. no. 6088.
Pen and wash, sepia and watercolour retouched in Indian ink; 448 x 303 mm.
Inscr.: above, 'Sepolcro dei Eccel. mi Valier a S. Gio: e Polo a Venezia del Proto Sig: Tirali'.
Prov.: De Marinis 1915. *Lit.:* Bassi, 1962 and 1963; Zava Boccazzi, 1965; Brusatin, 1980.
This fine unpublished drawing by Andrea Tirali refers to the large funerary monument raised to the Valier family in the first decade of the eighteenth century.

The architect Antonio Gaspari had already prepared some designs for this tomb, in accordance with the will drawn up in 1696 by Doge Silvestro Valier, the son of Doge Bertucci. However, these were replaced by Tirali's project, which partly incorporated Gaspari's suggestions. The three statues show the figures of the Doges and of Bertucci's wife, Elisabetta Querini.

Tirali's drawing shows some, possibly fundamental, variations from the finished monument, especially in the *oculus* above. However, the nature and arrangement of the luxuriant sculptural effect already seems substantially defined. The sculptors who carried out the designs were among the best of those active in Venice from the end of the seventeenth to the beginning of the eighteenth centuries: Giovanni Bonazza, Pietro Baratta, Antonio Tarsia, possibly Marino Groppelli and some others. The Valier tomb was one of the most significant monuments produced in Venice during these years, and shows a scenographic spirit and an austere monumental effect. The monument abandons the Longhenian taste for the spectacular and many of the late-seventeenth century displays of rhetorical agitation in the style of Gaspari, and reveals a significant, severely oratorical and heroic dimension (Bertucci had been Doge at the time of the Venetian victory over the Turks at the Dardanelles in 1657). On the other hand, Tirali is himself regarded as the architect who started the late-Classical and broadly Palladian revision of Venetian architecture that was to lead, with Temanza and his followers, to the neoclassical reformulation of the language of building.

Sebastiano Ricci (1659-1734)
22. *The Continence of Scipio*
Inv. no. 1774.
Pen and sepia and wash on yellowish paper;
167 x 228 mm.
Inscr.: 'Scipione romano', 'Ricci' (in the
artist's hand).
Prov.: Gamba, 1841. *Lit.:* Pignatti, 1959,
p. 192; Idem, 1963, no. 1; Idem, 1964, no. 1;
Idem, 1968, no. 1.
Exhibitions: Venice, Seicento, 1959, no. 102;
USA, 1963, no. 1.
This striking sketch illustrates the artist's
graphic style at the start of the eighteenth
century, when he painted many versions of a
subject. A painting at Hampton Court is
closely related to this sketch (Blunt, 1946,
p. 267; Levey, 1964, no. 641, pl. 96). A
variation of the subject, datable around
1713-16, is at Chatsworth (publ. by Orti, in
Commentarii, 1951, 133). This drawing seems
to be also an 'idea' for the painting of the
same subject at Parma University, datable
around the end of the century. The drawing's
style is reminiscent of Giordano and
Solimena and confirms the influence of
Ricci's early experiences in Naples and
Florence. In these early sheets Ricci's graphic
style appears to be still tied to the Baroque
tradition, both for the masterly planned and
solemn composition and the hatching,
suggesting a rich pictorial effect. However,
there are already some elements that mark
the transition towards that looser and
quivering graphic style which foretells the
artistic evolution taking place at the beginning of the following century. A similar
evolution can be seen in Ricci's paintings, if
one compares the Hampton Court and
Parma pictures with the later version of the
same subject which Ricci painted in the
Marucelli Palace in Florence, in 1706.

Gaspare Diziani
23. *A Decorative Fountain with Putti and a Figure of an Old Man*
Inv. no. 972.
Pen and brown ink, and sepia wash; 210 x 223 mm.
Prov.: Correr, 1830. *Lit.:* Pignatti, 1959, 451; Idem, 1964, no. 60.
Exhibitions: Groningen, 1964, no. 60.
A large number of drawings by Diziani have been in the past attributed to other artists, such as Crosara, Guarana, and Pellegrini. Pignatti (1959, 451; 1964, no. 60) gave this sheet to Pellegrini, finding some stylistic similarities with another sheet by the artist,

Darius's body carried in front of Alexander, which is in the Mauritshuis Museum, The Hague (Bettagno, 1959, no. 65). The two drawings have in effects a dramatic tension in common, but we tend now to accept Martini's attribution of the present sheet, together with a large number of others originally ascribed to Pellegrini, to Gaspare Diziani (Martini, 1983, p. 524).

Jacopo Amigoni (1682-1752)
24. Portrait of a Gentleman
Inv. no. 737.
Black chalk and sepia wash, heightened with
white; grey paper on white sheet, on grey
supporting sheet; 230 x 158 mm.
Prov.: Correr, 1830. *Lit.:* Pignatti, 1963,
no. 13; Idem, 1964, no. 13; Idem, 1965,
no. 13; Idem, 1965, no. 12; Idem, 1973,
no. 29; Idem, 1980, no. 3.
Exhibitions: Washington, 1963, no. 13;
Venice, 1964, no. 13.
The Correr collection owns two portrait
drawings of this type, both attributed to
Amigoni's English period (1729-39). From
the stylistical and technical point of view,
however, neither of them can be related to a
series of drawings on blue paper which have
been attributed to Amigoni's English period.
These 44 sheets are now dispersed in many
collections, such as the Princeton University
Museum, with five portraits, the Scholz
collection, the Stockholm Museum, the
British Museum and the Louvre (Elaine
Claye, 1974, pp. 41-48). This series of
drawings is certainly related to paintings
belonging to Amigoni's English period, but it
is not necessarily by him. It was part of a
sketchbook which was taken apart by the
antique-dealer Meatyard in 1925. Another
more consistent group of drawings is recorded
as being in the possession of J.G. Lousada in
1933, and it was subsequently sold.

According to Watson, in the sketchbook
there was not any attribution of the drawings
to Amigoni. There was only a print of
Amigoni's portrait of Empress Catherine of
Russia, which was bound together with the
drawings: undoubtedly very insignificant
evidence if one considers that the portrait
was executed after the English period and
therefore the related print was inserted in the
sketchbook after its execution. According to
Watson, who reports also a similar opinion
by Oppè, the blue paper sketchbook seemed
to be a sort of itinerant portrait painter's
album, used for giving the sitters an idea of
the possible compositions and poses (this
explains also the existence of the print of
Amigoni's royal portrait).

Edward Croft-Murray has already put
forward an attribution to the Englishman
Thomas Hudson (Bjurstroem, 1962, 220),
and we are inclined to accept his suggestion,
owing also to the discovery of an original
inscription 'T. Hudson del. t.' which appears
in two drawings of the series (Claye, cit.
nos. 29-34)

Gian Antonio Guardi (1699-1760)
25. *The Triumph of Virtue*
Inv. no. 8221.
Black pencil, pen and brush and brown ink;
290 x 409 mm.
Inscr.: 'La Virtù Guerriera trionfante/tirata
dal Tempo/che la conduce al Tempio/con la
Fama che la corona/di lauro e la compagna/
con la tromba' (pencil, in the artist's hand);
'Giouan Antonio Guardi Veneto Pitore'
(pencil, in the artist's hand on the verso).
Prov.: Meissner; Morassi, 1966. *Lit.:* Morassi,
1953, 263; Moschini, 1956, 10; Pignatti,
1957, 29, no. 11; Parker–Byam Shaw, 1962,
48, no. 10; Fiocco, 1965, 14; Pallucchini,
1965, 223; Pignatti, 1965, 154, no. 18;
Zampetti, 1965, 307; Dania, 1966, 293;
Pignatti, 1967, 17/19, 23, 24; Idem, 1967,
VII; Sinding Larsen, 1967, 201; Dania, 1968,
30; Morassi, 1968, 136; Zampetti, 1969, 252,
no. 113; Bettagno, 1971, 72, no. 149; Idem,
1972, 60, no. 112; Morassi, 1975, 86-87,
no. 40; Byam Shaw, 1976, 857; Binion, 1976,
188; Dessins Vénitiens, 1983, 159.
Exhibitions: Paris, 1960-61; Venice, 1965;
Venice, 1969; Paris, 1971; London, 1972;
Bruxelles, 1983.

A real masterpiece of Gian Antonio Guardi's
graphic production, this drawing is undoubtedly by him. The artist's style shows the
influence of Pellegrini and, in part, of
Tiepolo, achieving an harmonious composition for a ceiling decoration. Dania's very
recent discovery of other drawings of the
same series in the Fermo Library and in
Paris confirms the fact that these sheets had
the function of modelli (Morassi, 1975,
nos. 41-44). All the figures are familiar to us:
from the Virtue which anticipates the Cini
Aurora and the Ca 'Rezzonico *Diana*, to the
putti interlacing garlands, similar to those of
the Belvedere altarpiece. From the latter in
particular derives the dating around 1746, in
spite of controversial opinions (Fiocco, 1965,
14: 'if not the first one, one of the first
drawings by Gian Antonio'). The stylistic
closeness to the *Madonna and Saints* (Morassi,
1975, no. 13), also related to the Belvedere
painting, confirms our dating. In this sheet
there are very important indications of Gian
Antonio's style, always bound to a technical
virtuosity: the pen strokes are soft and loose;
the surfaces are broken by serpentine and
zig-zag-like touches (see the angel's drapery
and wing); the contours of the hands and the
faces are reinforced with a darker line (umber
is usually used in the paintings); the figures'
curly hair is fluently drawn using the brush
with capricious grace, like that of Christ in
the Pasiano altarpiece, or of Tobiah and
Sarah in the panels of the Angelo Raffaele.

Gian Antonio Guardi
26. *Madonna and Child with Three Saints*
Red pencil, pen and sepia, and sepia wash on yellowish paper; 360 x 220 mm.
Prov.: Marius Paulme (Lugt, 1910); Antonio Morassi collection, Milan (loan 1983; Lugt 143a). *Lit.:* Morassi, 1953, p. 261; Pignatti, 1957; p. 25; Byam-Shaw, 1962, p. 48; Pignatti, 1963, no. 5; Idem, 1964, no. 5.
Exhibitions: Fondazione Cini, Venice, 1962, no. 53.
This extraordinary sheet, in deposit from the Morassi collection, is certainly related to the Belvedere altarpiece, probably painted in 1746, and it is one of Gian Antonio's masterpieces.

The airy and zig-zag-line composition, the fluent touch and the shining and gold-like colour effects show the fundamental characters of Gian Antonio's style.

Nicola Grassi (1682-1748)
27. *Fallen Christ*
Inv. no. 5558-5559.
Red and white chalk on brown paper; 300 x 448 mm.
Prov.: Molin, 1885. *Lit.:* Coggiola Pittoni, 1934, 263 (attr. to Pittoni); Pignatti, 1963, no. 7; Idem, 1964, no. 7; Idem, 1965, no. 7; Idem, 1965, 159; Binion, 1983, 79 (Pittoni with reserve); Pignatti, 1984, 74; Pignatti, 1983, no. 499.
Exhibitions: Washington, 1963; Venice, 1964; London, 1965.
Verso: Fallen Christ
Black pencil.
Given to the Correr with an old attribution to Gaspare Diziani and by Coggiola Pittoni (1934, 263) as a work by Pittoni, this drawing is one of the most interesting works of Nicola Grassi's graphic catalogue. It was first ascribed to Grassi by Pignatti (1963, no. 7). Recent studies (Pignatti, cat. 1982) have attributed about ten drawings to the artist, stressing the fact that his style has been gradually changing from an early period influenced by Cameo's manner to an intermediate one between Crespi and Piazzetta

and finally to a later one influenced by Pittoni and Ricci. And just to this last period – dating around the 1740s and 50s – belongs the Correr sheet, in which Grassi's aggressive handling is expressed by a nervous line, different from Pittoni's less dramatic style. While Binion still ascribes no. 27, though 'with some reserve', to Pittoni (1983, 79), Pignatti points out that there are many elements in favour of the sheet's attribution to Grassi, as the clear closeness to the *Study of a Male Nude* in the Metropolitan Museum, New York (Pignatti, fig. 7) or to the picture of the Buttò collection in Pordenone (Rizzi, 1968, p. 25).

Giambattista Pittoni (1687-1767)
28. *Allegory of Fame*
Inv. no. 6067.
Red pencil and wash on yellowish paper;
171 x 78 mm.
Prov.: Fontana. *Lit.:* Pignatti, 1963, no. 9;
Byam Shaw, 1964, p. 178; Pignatti, 1964,
no. 9; Pignatti, 1965, no. 9.
Exhibitions: USA, 1963, no. 9.
Verso: Sketch of the Same Subject
Red pencil on grey paper.
This drawing, probably for a ceiling decor-
ation, is related to other compositional

sketches, such as Correr nos. 1368 and 1365,
although no such composition in oil is known
(Pallucchini, 1945, p. 66, figs. 10 and 11).
The wavy lines and painterly washes are
reminiscent of Pittoni's best paintings
around 1730.

Giambattista Pittoni
29. *The Adoration of the Shepherds*
Inv. no. 784.
Pencil heightened with white on brown
paper; 182 x 97 mm.
Prov.: Correr, 1830. *Lit.:* Pallucchini, 1945,

p. 105; Pignatti, 1963, no. 10; Byam Shaw,
1964, p. 178; Pignatti, 1964, no. 10; Idem,
1965, no. 10.
Exhibitions: USA, 1963, no. 10.
This drawing is connected with a fine oil
sketch in Count Seilern's collection, London
(Seilern, 1959, p. 66, pl. LXXI). The Correr
owns four of these small compositions,
which are probably records of, rather than
studies for, paintings, but were no doubt
drawn by the artist himself.

Giovanni Battista Pittoni
30. *Study of Nine Heads*
Inv. no. 5407.
Red chalk on tracing paper; 353 x 245 mm.
Prov.: Molin, 1813. *Lit.:* Coggiola Pittoni,
1934, p. 4, fig. 4; Pallucchini, 1945, p. 80,
no. 55; Binion, 1983, p. 78, fig. 345.
Coggiola Pittoni *(op. cit.)* and Pallucchini
(op. cit.) have both attributed this drawing to
Pittoni.

Coggiola Pittoni suggests that the third
head on the left (from the top) is quite close to
that of the boy who gives some bread to an
old man in the *Feeding of the Five Thousand* in
the Accademia Galleries in Venice, while the
one next to it is reminiscent of the page's
head in the *Adoration of the Magi* in the church
of SS. Nazario e Celso, Brescia.

Binion *(op. cit.)* states that the attribution
of this sheet is rather difficult, because its
style could be ascribed both to Pittoni and to
Kern. Therefore she gives the drawing to
Pittoni with some reserve. According to her,
some heads are connected with paintings
dated from around the 1730s. The first head
on the left (from the top) corresponds, in
reverse, to the figure of the warrior in the
painting with the *Sacrifice of Polissena* in the
Louvre and the second one on the right (from
the top) to that of the standard-bearer in the
same painting. The second head on the right
(from the bottom) corresponds to that of a
boy in the *Feeding of the Five Thousand* and
also to that of the boy with a candle in the
Circumcision, both in the Accademia
Galleries, Venice.

The head wearing a turban on the bottom
left is the same of two other drawings in a
private collection, Padua (Pallucchini, 1945,
nos. 39 and 40).

71

Anton Kern (1710-1737)
31. *A Girl with Doves*
Inv. no. 5461.
Red chalk on brown paper; 440 x 320 mm.
Prov.: Molin, 1813. *Lit.:* Pallucchini, 1945,
p. 102, no. 123; Pignatti, 1964, no. 73; Idem,
1965, no. 27; Zava Boccazzi, 1975, pp. 248-
249; Binion, 1983, p. 85.
Exhibitions: Groningen, 1964, no. 73.
This drawing was first attributed to Pittoni
by Pallucchini (1945, *op. cit.*) and then Binion
(1964, *op. cit.*). Zava Boccazzi (1975, *op. cit.*)
and then Binion (1983, *op. cit.*), on the other
hand, suggested the attribution to Kern,
which is now generally accepted. Anton
Kern was in Pittoni's workshop from 1725 to
1734, before leaving Venice and going to
Prague.

Gaspare Diziani (1689-1797)
32. *The Flight into Egypt*
Inv. no. 5631.
Red pencil, pen and sepia, and sepia wash, on
yellowish paper; 210 x 415 mm.
Inscr.: 'nero' (pen, in the artist's hand).
Prov.: Molin, 1855. *Lit.:* Derschau, 1922,
p. 157, tav. 134; Coletti, 1935, p. 528; Fenyo,
1959, p. 91; Pignatti, 1963, no. 16; Idem,
1964, no. 16; Idem, 1965, no. 19; Zampetti,
1969, no. 107; Zugni Tauro, 1971, p. 91,
fig. 344; Pignatti, 1973, no. 35; Idem, 1981,
no. 249.
Exhibitions: Washington, 1963, no. 16;
Venice, 1964, no. 16; London, 1965, no. 19;
Venice, 1969, no. 107.
This is, as pointed out by Pignatti, a preparatory sketch for the large canvas in the
Sacristy of S. Stefano, Venice. A 'modelletto'
(or finished sketch for submission to the
patron) is in a private collection in Bologna,
but the drawing is closer to the painting,
dated from 1733. Comparing this drawing to
earlier ones – such as *Mary and Elizabeth*
(Correr no. 5518), dated from 1713 and
executed in Belluno, or two studies of bearded
heads (Correr nos. 5533-35), inscribed
'Dresda Polonia', which dates them before
his return to Venice in 1720 – Diziani's
draughtsmanship shows its evolution from
late Baroque chiaroscuro washes in the
manner of his teacher, Gregorio Lazzarini,
through a hatching technique and a crispness
of style influenced by Ricci, to a painterly
Rococo style related to that of Pellegrini and
G.A. Guardi. The medium is characteristic
of Diziani's large preparatory drawings.

It must be noted that in the drawing, and
therefore in the painting, there are all the
compositional elements that Sebastiano
Ricci had already depicted in his *Flight into
Egypt* in Bakewell (Daniels, 1976, no. 9,
fig. 10).

73

of this work in the artist's mature period is not therefore too daring, though considering that Gaspare has always been particularly inclined towards Pellegrini's manner during his whole lifetime. Of the same opinion is B. Aikema (1981).

Gaspare Diziani
34. *Annunciation*
Inv. no. 5532.
Red pencil, pen and sepia, and sepia wash: 410 x 290 mm.
Prov.: Molin, 1855. *Lit.:* Pignatti, 1963. no. 19; Idem, 1964, no. 19; Idem, 1965. no. 22; Zampetti, 1969, no. 109; Pignatti, 1981, no. 314.
Exhibitions: Washington, 1963, no. 19; Venice, 1964, no. 19; London, 1965, no. 22; Venice, 1969, no. 109.
This drawing is related to the painting in the Belluno Museum, executed between 1750 and 1755 (Zugni Tauro, 1971, pl. 156), whose composition is the same but in reverse. The drawing, as pointed out by Pignatti, (1964, no. 19), reveals unexpected analogies with Pellegrini's style and is a late work by Diziani.

The Correr Museum owns a large number of sheets with this subject-matter; very similar to this one, but probably a bit earlier, is no. 963. In the Albertina there is another drawing which is very similar to the Correr one; it was formerly attributed to Ricci (Stix-Fröchlich-Bum, 1926, no. 238) and more recently to Fontebasso by Benesh in the Venetian exhibition of 1961 (no. 96). In his review of the exhibition, Fiocco supported the attribution to Gaspare Diziani of the Albertina drawing (1961, p. 320); and the attribution was, in effect, accepted in the new catalogue of the Albertina (Koschatzky, Oberhüber, Knab, 1972, fig. 52).

Gaspare Diziani
33. *The Judgement of Paris*
Inv. no. 5508.
Pen and sepia, and sepia wash; 253 x 194 mm.
Prov.: Molin, 1855. *Lit.:* Bettagno, 1959, no. 105 (G.A. Pellegrini); Pignatti, 1959, p. 452 (G.A. Pellegrini); Valcanover, 1960, no. 349 (G.A. Pellegrini); Pignatti, 1963, no. 3 (G.A. Pellegrini); Idem, 1964, no. 3 (G.A. Pellegrini); Byam Shaw, 1964, p. 177, no. 3 (G. Diziani); Pignatti, 1973, no. 38 (G. Diziani); Idem, 1981, no. 351 (G. Diziani).
Exhibitions: Venice, 1959, no. 105; Washington, 1963, no. 3; Venice, 1964, no. 3.
This drawing has been attributed to Pellegrini for a long time; Byam Shaw first suggested the young Diziani under the influence of Pellegrini. Pignatti pointed out some similarities between the central and the reclining figures of the drawing and the two same figures depicted in the *Hercules and Omphale* in the Musée d'Art et d'Histoire, Geneva, dated around 1750-1760 (Zugni Tauro, 1971, pl. 245), where nevertheless the central figure's pose is reversed. Pignatti noted also the close relationship between the Correr drawing and the *Alexander and Darius* in the Mauritshuis, The Hague, work by Pellegrini dated around 1717-18.

The analogy with the Geneva *Hercules and Omphale*, suggested by Pignatti, seems to be very relevant as far as the graphic style and the subject-matter are concerned; the placing

75

Gaspare Diziani
35. *Rinaldo and Armida*
Inv. no. 5632-33.
Pen and sepia; 300 x 515 mm.
Prov.: Molin, 1855. *Lit.:* Pignatti, 1981, no. 290.
There are no known paintings to which the drawing can be related. The parallel hatching suggests a close dating to the frescoes of Palazzo Riccati now Avogadro degli Azzoni in Castelfranco Veneto; the Museo Correr owns two preparatory sketches of the frescoes (Inv. nos. 5571-72, cat. no. 283).

Gaspare Diziani
36. *Two Bissona Costumes*
Inv. no. 5791a.
Black pencil, pen and sepia, and coloured washes; 158 x 220 mm.
Inscr.: 'Le Scienze n. 10 barcaroli n. 6 sonatori; Arti n. 10 baracaroli 6 sonatori' (pen, in the artist's hand); Gasp. Diziani (in a nineteenth century hand).
Prov.: Vason. *Lit.:* Pignatti, 1963, no. 22; Idem, 1964, no. 22; Idem, 1965, no. 27; Zugni Tauro, 1971, p. 94, pl. 350; Pignatti, 1973, no. 36; Romanelli–Pedrocco, 1980, no. 75; Pignatti, 1981, no. 421.
Exhibitions: Washington, 1963, no. 22; Venice, 1964, no. 22; London, 1965, no. 27; Venice, 1980, no. 75.
A charming drawing (one of two in the Correr) showing costume studies for two oarsmen, representing the Sciences and the Arts. They were evidently prepared for a Carnival Bissona, a special boat used for festivals in Venice. Although no similar drawings by Diziani are known, this attribution is suggested by such a painting as the artist's *Festival of Sta. Marta* (Ca' Rezzonico, no. 115), which also indicates an interest in subjects of this genre (Pignatti, 1973, no. 36). As the painting dates from the artist's late period, the same dating would be appropriate for the drawing.

Jacopo Guarana (1720-1808)
37. *Venus Triumphant*
Inv. no. 5473.
Brush and grey ink, and tempera, on yellowish paper; 330 x 440 mm.
Prov.: Molin, 1813. *Lit.:* Pignatti, 1963, no. 34; Idem, 1964, no. 34; Idem, 1965, no. 41.
A sketch for a ceiling decoration which can be easily related to some bozzetti by the artist in the Villa Pisani at Strà (*Time and Glory* for instance). The muted colours and the balanced composition are typical of Guarana, while the clear reminiscences of Diziani belong to his cultural background.

Francesco Fontebasso (1709-1769)
38. *The Death of St. Mary Magdalene*
Inv. no. 6562.
Black pencil, pen and brown ink, and brown wash, heightened with white; 480 x 350 mm.
Prov.: Cini, 1935. *Lit.:* Lorenzetti, 1935, 153, no. 24; Pignatti, 1973, fig. 33; Idem, 1981, no. 470.
There is a copy in Washington, National Gallery (Inv. B-26-748). The copyist, it should be noted, has used parallel hatching to convey the chiaroscuro washes in the original, of typical Tiepolesque derivation. The comparison between the two sheets suggests a certain inclination towards Northern prototypes; the technique creates bright, shot-like effects, more reminiscent of Rubens than the Venetian school.

Gregorio Lazzarini (1655-1730)
39. *A Saint in Glory*
Inv. no. 5724.
Black pencil, pen and black ink, and grey
wash; 163 x 123 mm.
Inscr.: 'Lazarini' (in an eighteenth-century
hand); 'n. 19'.
Prov.: Molin, 1813. *Lit.:* Muraro, 1953, 44;
Pignatti, 1959, no. 87; Idem, 1965, no. 6.
Exhibitions: Venice, 1959, no. 87.
The attribution of this drawing to Lazzarini
appears fairly certain and the sketch can be
related to the signed *Fall of Mannah* in the
Ambrosiana, Milan (Ivanoff, *Gerolamo
Pellegrini*, in Emporium, 1958, no. 103,
p. 106). The Saint shown here is perhaps
S. Lorenzo Giustiniani, and the drawing
might also refer to the large canvas by
Lazzarini in S. Pietro di Castello, Venice. In
any case, I would place the drawing in the
eighteenth century: it has obvious affinities
with the art of Giordano, whose influence is
also apparent in the early work of the young
G.B. Tiepolo when he was a pupil of
Lazzarini.

Mattia Bortoloni (1696-1750)
40. *Susannah and the Elders*
Inv. no. 5696.
Pen and grey ink, and wash, on yellowish
paper; 253 x 220 mm.
Inscr.: 'Bortoloni' (possibly in the artist's
hand).
Prov.: Molin, 1885. *Lit.:* Pignatti, 1963,
no. 23; Idem, 1964, no. 23; Idem, 1965,
no. 29; Idem, 1965, no. 40; Idem, 1980,
no. 49.
Exhibitions: Washington, 1963, no. 23;
Venice, 1964, no. 23; London, 1965, no. 29.
On the basis of late works such as the ceiling
of San Bartolomeo, Bergamo, or the frescoes
of the Villa Visconti at Brignano, Ivanoff
affirms that Bortoloni 'suffers Tiepolo's
temptation' (1957, p. 12). This is a valid
remark, even though the Bertarelli *Alexander
the Great*, adduced as an example, is quite
controversial, considering that his attribution
to Bortoloni is founded mainly upon the

inscription, while the style is a bit too much
rococo and rather reminiscent of Diziani.

This drawing showing Susannah seems to
confirm that Bortoloni's style, after the very
early influence of Balestra, moved towards a
Riccesque and then Tiepolesque manner.
The zig-zag-lines and the pictorial washes of
this sheet are in effects reminiscent of
Pellegrini and suggest therefore a dating
around 1730.

The attribution to Bortoloni is further
confirmed by the comparison with the
Judgment of Paris in the Ashmolean Museum,
Oxford, which bears the inscription of the
'Ignoto Collezionista Veneziano', who vary
rarely fails in his judgments (Bettagno, 1966,
no. 79).

Gerolamo Brusaferro (1680-1790)
41. *Agar and Ishmael in the Desert with the Angel*
Inv. no. 978.
Black pencil, pen and brown ink and sepia wash; 236 x 180 mm.
Prov.: Correr, 1830. *Lit.:* Pignatti, 1980, no. 50.

Brusaferro's graphic production (he was in Venice, registered in the Painter's Guild, from 1702 to 1721, and active in Santo Stefano in 1737) is by now well known, thanks to recent studies. His style, showing the influence of Ricci and Pellegrini, is documented by examples bearing old inscriptions, such as those in the Sholz collection, in the British Museum, in the Cabinet des Estampes, Paris, in the Academy of Fine Arts, Vienna, in the Albertina, all mentioned by Bettagno (1966, nos. 115-117).

   This fine drawing is very close to the Budapest sheet (Fenyo, 1965, no. 86), both iconographically, for the angel's and boy's figures, and stylistically, for the silvery tonality which is reminiscent of Pellegrini in the years 1720-30.

Giambattista Crosato (1697-1756)
42. *Zephyrus and Flora*
Inv. no. 960.
Pen and sepia ink, and sepia wash, on grey paper; 346 x 172 mm.
Prov.: Correr, 1830. *Lit.:* Pignatti, 1963, no. 15; Idem, 1964, no. 15; Idem, 1965, no. 15; Idem, 1980, no. 219; Idem, 1973, no. 51.
Exhibitions: Washington, 1963, no. 15; Venice, 1964, no. 15; London, 1965, no. 15. In his monograph of 1941 Fiocco was the first to point out a group of drawings that, according to old inscriptions or stylistic elements, seemed to him quite close to Crosato's work, known at that time only for his pictorial production. Fiocco, however, did not know this drawing, which was later identified by Pignatti (1963, no. 15), and whose attribution is now fully confirmed by Bettagno, who points out three drawings bearing the always reliable inscription of the Ignoto Collezionista Veneziano (1966, no. 80-81 and 175). From the stylistic point of view this sheet is also related to the

St. Charles Borromeus of the Seilern collection (1959, no. 27).
Zephyrus resembles a youth holding a bow in the fresco of Phaeton Room in the Stupinigi Hunting Casino (1731-32), while the foreshortening of the putto and the cornice with the giant vase appear in the frescoes of the Villa della Regina, Turin, dated from 1733 (in Fiocco, 1959, figs. 9 and 20). Crosato's connections with Ricci and Diziani are even more interesting after this identification.

Giambattista Marcuola (1711-80)
43. *The Victory of Cyrus*
Inv. no. 5226.
Red pencil, pen and sepia, and sepia wash; 298 x 398 mm.
Prov.: Bosa. *Lit.:* Pignatti, 1963, no. 26; Idem, 1964, no. 26; Idem, 1965, no. 31; Idem, 1968, no. 43.
The signed drawings in the Hermitage, Leningrad (Dobroklousky, 1951, pl. XCV), can be used as a guide to further attributions. Because of obvious similarities with the Hermitage sheet, this sketch can be ascribed to the same artist.
This drawing is certainly by the same hand of the one in the Cini Foundation, Venice (Bettagno, 1963, no. 46), which is signed; the figure on the right is almost identical to that of the soldier who offers Pompey's head to Caesar.

Giuseppe Bazzani (1690-1769)
44. *The Ascension*
Inv. no. 8297.
Black pencil; 200 x 150 mm.
Prov.: Musatti, 1967. *Lit.:* Pignatti, 1970-71,
no. 22; Idem, 1980, no. 33.
Exhibitions: Venice, 1970, no. 22.
For composition and type this drawing is
close to several figures of Bazzani's paintings,
such as the Carli *Ascension*, Ravenna, and the
Assumption in the Verona Museum (in
Ivanoff, 1950, figs. 26 and 76). The soft and
impasto-like handling is similar to that of the
Heads in the Budapest Museum (repr. in
Puppi, 1962, fig. 39), rather than of other
drawings less convincingly attributed to
Bazzani (Ivanoff, 1950, figs. 74, 75 and 83).

Gerolamo Mauro (1725-1766)
45. *Study for a Festival Bissona*
Inv. no. 7314.
Pen and sepia ink and coloured washes on
traces of black pencil; 312 x 460 mm.
Inscr.: 'L'Adria condotta in trionfo da Venere
dea del Mar/ è Tetti sua compagna' (in pen,
in an eighteenth-century hand).
Lit: Damerini, 1912, 52; Lorenzetti, 1936,
no. 15; Idem, 1937, 42, no. 15; Byam Shaw,
1937, 18; Pallucchini, 1943, 52, no. 102;
Arslan, 1944, 9 (not in the artist's hand);
Catalogue of the Zurich exhibition, 1958, 32,
no. 289; Pignatti, 1964, 30-1, no. 42; Morassi,
1975, 131, no. 305 (probably by an imitator);
Romanelli-Pedrocco, 1980, 21, no. 73
(Girolamo II Mauro ?).
Exhibitions: Venice, 1937, no. 15; Zurich,
1955, no. 144; Munich, 1958, no. 289;
Groningen, 1964, no. 42; Venice, 1980,
no. 73.

Pier Leone Ghezzi (1674-1755)
46. *Don Gennaro Duke of Medina*
Inv. no. 8289.
Pen and brush and brown ink; 320 x 225 mm.
Inscr.: 'Don Gennaro duca di Medina' (pen,
in the artist's hand).
Prov.: Musatti, 1967. *Lit.:* Pignatti, 1970-71,
no. 28; Idem, 1983, no. 487.
Exhibitions: Venice, 1970.
This sheet belongs to a group of seven
drawings by Pier Leone Ghezzi bequeathed
to the Correr Museum by Riccardo Musatti
in 1967. The sheets are very similar in style
and good examples of that cursive style
which characterizes the best caricatures by
the artist. There are other similar sheets in
the Boston Museum, in the Bick collection,
Longmeadow, Massachussets (Pignatti,
1970-71, no. 28; repr. in Robinson and

Paoletti, 1971, no. 36) and in a private
Roman collection (repr. in Abruzzese, 1955,
figs. 14 and 15). This type of caricature is
different in its free and rapid pen-strokes
which create a pictorial effect, from Ghezzi's
usually dry and hard graphic style, with
parallel pen-strokes (see the drawings in the
Albertina, the Vatican Library and the
British Museum); in them the artist succeeds
in communicating with greater effect his
subtle sense of humour.

All the seven drawings are ascribed to
Ghezzi's early period, before 1720, when the
artist's style becomes less creative and more
repetitive (Abruzzese, *op. cit.*, 307).

This is perhaps the best drawing by
Ghezzi owned by the Correr, for its lively
characterization of the Duke, by means of
loose and energetic pen-strokes.

Don Gennaro Casa di Medina

Federico Bencovich (*c.* 1677-1756)
47. *The Flight into Egypt*
Inv. no. 239.
Black pencil and red chalk; 475 x 378 mm.
Inscr.: 'Bencovich' (pen, in the artist's hand).
Prov.: Molin, 1885. *Lit.:* Pallucchini, 1932,
306; Idem, 1936, 318; Valcanover, 1954, 66;
Bettagno, 1963, no. 6; Pignatti, 1964, no. 3;
Idem, 1965, no. 8; Moretti, 1978, 108.
Exhibitions: Groningen, 1964, no. 3; London,
1965, no. 8.
The drawing, which bears the inscription
'Bencovich', was identified by Pallucchini in
1932. It was first considered an early work,
until Valcanover (1954) dated it around
1725, because of its relation, certainly a
preparatory sketch, to the painting of the
church of S. Giuseppe at Tomo, near Feltre,
published by him. Bencovich's style during
the 1720s is reminiscent of Piazzetta in its
mellow lightness, but it still retains the
substantial plasticity derived from his
Bolognese origins. A further element which
confirms the attribution to Bencovich is
given by the comparison with the academic
life studies which have been recently ascribed
to the artist. In particular the modelling of
St. Joseph's leg and arm recalls the handling
of the two sheets in the Castello Sforzesco
published by Precerutti Garberi (1971,
nos. 43-44). Also a certain tendency to
reinforce the outlines with charcoal –
emphasizing the highlights – appears in all
these sheets.

Giambattista Piazzetta (1683-1754)
48. *The Dead Christ and Four Saints*
Inv. no. 5682.
Black pencil heightened with white on grey
paper; 355 x 210 mm.
Prov.: Molin, 1813. *Lit.:* Pignatti, 1963,
no. 39; Idem, 1964, no. 39.
Exhibitions: Washington, 1963, no. 39;
Venice, 1964, no. 39.
This drawing is certainly a compositional
sketch and is typically Piazzettesque in its
lively composition, which rises with a zigzag movement towards the top, where the
angel flies above the clouds. The upper part
can be compared with the drawing of San
Vidal in the Correr (Pignatti, 1957, p. 397,
fig. 44), while the lower part with the saints is
quite similar to the *Assumption* belonging to
Janos Scholz, ascribed by Pallucchini to
Piazzetta despite Zanetti's erroneous attribution to Nicola Grassi.

Giovani Battista Piazzetta
49. *A Young Lady*
Inv. no. 1569.
Black pencil; 243 x 166 mm.
Inscr.: 'Piazzetta'.
Lit.: unpublished.
This is probably a preparatory study for the tailpiece of a book. In Piazzetta's œuvre these tailpieces were given a greater importance: they were often of large size and included figures and landscapes. Piazzetta's collaboration with the publisher and printer Albrizzi is well-known; collaboration which produced remarkable works such as the 1745 edition of Tasso's *Gerusalemme Liberata*.

Giambattista Piazzetta
50. *Portrait of a Young Man*
Inv. no. 1776.
Black and white chalk, on brownish paper; 346 x 284 mm.
Prov.: Correr, 1830. *Lit.:* Pignatti, 1963, no. 36; Idem, 1964, no. 36; Idem, 1965, no. 42.
Exhibitions: Washington, 1963, no. 36; Venice, 1964, no. 36; London, 1965, no. 42.
Even in his early years Piazzetta was famous for his drawings – made independently from his paintings – especially for his heads done in black and white chalk. Pallucchini (1956, p. 56) quotes evidence for this from Balestra, Anton Maria Zanetti and other artists and collectors from 1717 onwards. This portrait is a fine example of Piazzetta's style, probably of the 1730s. The characteristic use of highlights resembles that of the *Boy and a Girl with a Trap* in the Accademia, Venice hini, 1956, fig. 157).

Giambattista Piazzetta
51. *The Standard Bearer*
Inv. no. 7058.
Black and white chalk, on grey paper; 520 x 398 mm.
Prov.: Correr, 1830. *Lit.:* Pallucchini, 1934, pp. 58, 99, fig. 75; Pignatti, 1963, no. 37; Pignatti, 1964, no. 37; Idem, 1965, no. 43.
Exhibitions: Washington, 1963, no. 37; Venice, 1964, no. 37; London, 1965, no. 43.
One of the best large album drawings by Piazzetta, of the same subject as the painting now at Dresden. The drawing is a little earlier and suggests a date around 1740, because the same head with a large hat appears in the *Pastoral* in the Art Institute, Chicago.

Giuseppe Angeli (1709-1798)
52. *St. James*
Inv. no. 7047.
Coloured chalks on bluish-grey prepared paper; 548 x 415 mm.
Prov.: Mayer, 1947 (?). *Lit.:* Pignatti, 1980, no. 11.
The affected pose and the pastel-like and shaded tones are very close to those of the Ca' Rezzonico St. James (inv. no. 1666, Pignatti, 1960, no. 20), formerly identified by Pallucchini as St. Roch and dated by him around 1750 (1931, 427).

Francesco Cappella (1714-1784)
53. *A Peasant Girl*
Inv. no. 378.
Black and white chalk on grey paper; 484 x 370 mm.
Prov.: Correr, 1830. *Lit.:* Pallucchini, 1932, p. 324; Idem, 1956, p. 50; Pignatti, 1963, no. 45; Idem, 1964, no. 45; Idem, 1965, no. 51; Idem, 1973, no. 47; Ruggeri, 1976, 42; Idem, 1977, 182; Pignatti, 1980, no. 62.
Exhibitions: Washington, 1963, no. 45; Venice, 1964, no. 45; London, 1965, no. 51.
Verso: Sketch of a Female Head
Black chalk.
Inscr.: 'Correr' (in a nineteenth-century hand).
In recent studies the catalogue of Cappella's drawings comprises more than 35 numbers (Ruggeri, 1977, pp. 179-182). It includes compositional sketches, whose hatching is often entangled but very expressive, figure studies and album drawings, so typical of Piazzetta's workshop. This peasant girl, on whose verso there is another very rapid sketch, is of such a great quality that Pallucchini – who had first given it to Cappella (1932, 324) – subsequently transferred it to Piazzetta (1956, 50). I still believe that the artist is Cappella, and this is confirmed by comparing the figure on the verso with other similar ones in the Accademia Carrara, Bergamo (Ragghianti, 1963, pp. 35-36). Recently the attribution to Cappella is confirmed by Ruggeri, too (1978, 182).

Cappella's style, with its rich colours and its charming iconography, developed already during his Bergamasque period, to which this drawing belongs.

The *Liberal Arts* painted in the Albani Bonomi palace in 1757-58 are in fact very close to the loose and soft handling of this sheet, where the chalk strokes are by no means different from Piazzetta's great incisiveness of light.

Domenico Maggiotto (1713-1793)
54. *A Peasant Girl in Profile*
Inv. no. 1617.
Black chalk, heightened with white, on blue-grey paper; 345 x 275 mm.
Prov.: Correr, 1830. *Lit.:* Pallucchini, 1932, pp. 492, 495, fig. 10; Pignatti, 1963, no. 43; Idem, 1964, no. 43; Idem, 1965, no. 49.
This is the companion piece to the *Head of a Priest*, also in the Correr (inv. no. 1620). It closely resembles a drawing at Windsor entitled *Girl in Contemplation*; the model appears to be the same (Blunt, 1957, p. 29, no. 43). As the Windsor drawings are dated around the 1730s, the present example is perhaps one of the earliest works by Maggiotto, drawn from life, when he was a young assistant in Piazzetta's workshop.

Egidio Dall'Oglio (1785-1784)
55. *St. Joseph and the Infant Christ*
Inv. no. 1643.
Prov.: Correr, 1830. *Lit.:* Pallucchini, 1932,
pp. 30, 34, fig. 7; Pignatti, 1963, no. 41; Idem,
1964, no. 41; Idem, 1965, no. 47; Idem, 1965,
no. 43, p. 174; Idem, 1981, no. 223.
Exhibitions: Washington, 1963, no. 41;
Venezia, 1964, no. 41; London, 1965, no. 47.
The correct attribution of sketches of heads
in the style of Piazzetta is often a difficult
matter. Many are in fact by the master's
followers, who imitate his style almost
perfectly, and the interpretation of quality is
not always enough for the correct attribution.
This drawing has been first attributed to
Marinetti (Pallucchini, 1932), but in 1963
was given by Pignatti *(op. cit.)* to the oldest of
Piazzetta's assistants, Egidio Dall'Oglio.
Dall'Oglio's modelling is hard and sharp,
with an extensive use of white chalk for the
highlights; this clearly distinguishes his style
from that of his master. Piazzetta himself
made a drawing of the same subject in a
similar sheet, now in the Alverà Collection,
Venice.

The attribution to Dall'Oglio is further
confirmed by the Child's closeness to the
Peasant Girl of a painting rightly attributed to
the artist by Pallucchini, in a private collection, London (1955, 224, fig. 261).

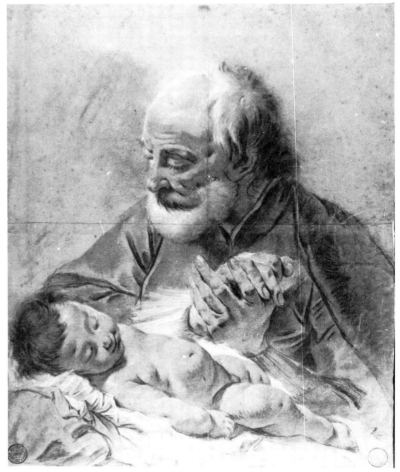

Giulia Lama (1681-1747)
56. *A Female Nude Leaning Against a Rock*
Inv. no. 6988.
Black chalk, heightened with white, on
yellowish paper; 440 x 572 mm.
Prov.: Donà dalle Rose collection. *Lit.:*
Ruggeri, 1973, pl. 182; Idem, 1973, 29.
This is one of a series of male and female nude
studies by Giulia Lama, which is owned by
the Correr Museum. It testifies to the artist's
attendance at the life drawing school run by
Giovan Battista Piazzetta, obviously a long
time before 1750, when he was given this
appointment by the Venetian Academy of
Fine Arts, and Giulia Lama was probably
dead.

The present drawing appears to be quite
close to some studies by Piazzetta, such as
the *Peasant Girl Getting Rid of Fleas*, formerly
in the Alverà collection, and the famous
Alverà *Nude* (Pallucchini, 1956, pls. 117 and
130), with its related drawings. Giulia
Lama's style, however, is different from
Piazzetta's in the soft lines and shading and
in the detail of the hands it is still reminiscent
of the young Tiepolo's drawings.

Giuseppe Nogari (1699-1763)
57. *Head of an Old Woman*
Inv. no. 742.
Black and red pencil, heightened with white,
on grey paper; 228 x 174 mm.
Prov.: Correr, 1830. *Lit.:* Pignatti, 1963,
no. 46; Idem, 1965, no. 52.
Exhibitions: Washington, 1963, no. 46;
Venice, 1964, no. 46; London, 1965, no.
52.
One of the few drawings attributed to Nogari,
who is better known as a pastel painter than
as a draughtsman. The attribution is based
on the *Boy's Head* in the Galleria Estense,
Modena (Pallucchini, 1933, p. 572, fig. 11). It
is interesting to note that this head was
discovered among the extensive Longhi
collection in the Correr, was acquired directly
from Alessandro Longhi. In his early years
Alessandro was Nogari's pupil.

Pietro Longhi (1702-1785)
58. *A Peasant with a Mandolin*
Inv. no. 557.
Black chalk, heightened with white, on
brown paper; 409 x 277 mm.
Prov.: Correr, 1830. *Lit.:* Pignatti, 1968,
p. 126; Idem, 1975, no. 2a.
Exhibitions: Venice, 1975, no. 2a.
Most of Pietro Longhi's handsome drawings
are related to paintings and were made as
studies for them. This drawing is connected
with a painting in the Ca 'Rezzonico in
Venice, *The Spinner*; the same figure of the
peasant appears in the left foreground. The
heavy chiaroscuro and shading used to
model the forms and the rather accurate
rendering of detail are typical of Longhi's
early style and confirm the dating of the
painting around the 1740s (Valcanover,
1956, 25). In the sketch drawn from life the
highlights are stresed by the white chalk,
while in the painting the light effects are
more subdued.

Pietro Longhi
59. *A Lady Fanning a Gentleman*
Inv. no. 454.
Black chalk, heightened with white, on
brown paper; 290 x 432 mm.
Inscr.: 'cosi fiancegiata legiadra, letto' (in the
artist's hand).
Prov.: Correr, 1830.
Lit.: Moschini, 1956, fig. 41; Pignatti, 1963,
no. 50; Idem, 1964, no. 49; Idem, 1965,
no. 56.
Exhibitions: Washington, 1963, no. 50;
Venice, 1964, no. 49; London, 1965, no. 56.
This is a sketch drawn from life, as testified
by the inscription, which refers to something
'slender and pretty', probably the lady's
waist. The drawing dates from the 1750s, for
the similarities with some studies in the
Correr for *The Awakening*, at Windsor.

Pietro Longhi
60. *A Maid Leaning on the Back of a Chair and
a Sketch of Drapery.*
Inv. no. 480.
Black chalk, heightened with white, on
brown paper; 279 x 389 mm.
Prov.: Correr, 1830. *Lit.:* Pignatti, 1968,
p. 122, pl. 337.
No painting related to this charming sketch
from life is known.

Pietro Longhi
61. *Two Ladies Meeting*
Inv. no. 493.
Black chalk, heightened with white, on
brown paper; 275 x 385 mm.
Prov.: Correr, 1830. *Lit.:* Pignatti, 1968,
p. 123, pl. 344.
This drawing might be connected with the
painting entitled *the Game of Cards Inter-
rupted*, which is in a private collection,
Bergamo (Pignatti, 1968, p. 86, pl. 272). The
two ladies, however, are much more static in
the painting, while here their very liveliness
is rendered by Longhi's masterly touch. Note
the expressive use of chiaroscuro and white
highlights to model the forms.

Though the Bergamo painting dates from
around 1779, I would suggest an earlier
dating for the present sheet, around the
1760s.

Pietro Longhi
62. *A Lady Spinning*
Inv. no. 465.
Black chalk, heightened with white, on
brown paper; 280 x 385 mm.
Prov.: Correr, 1830. *Lit.:* Ravà, 1923, p. 139;
Bjurstroem, 1962, p. 230; Pignatti, 1963,
no. 49; Idem, 1964, no. 48; Idem, 1965,
no. 54.
Exhibitions: Washington, 1963, no. 49;
Venice, 1964, no. 48; London, 1965, no. 54.
No painting after this drawing is known, but
one probably did exist originally. There is an
etching by Flipart entitled *Avowal of Love*,
which shows a lady spinning and is inscribed
'Pietro Longhi pinxit'; the print dates from
before 1750. A painting after the print is in
the Ca' Rezzonico, Venice (no. 141). Both
the print and the painting are in reverse to
the present drawing.

Pietro Longhi
63. *A Child in a Small Chair, Two Sketches of a
Boy's Head and Shoulders, A Lady with a
Fan*
Inv. no. 507.
Black chalk, heightened with white, on
brown paper; 227 x 345 mm.
Prov.: Correr, 1830. *Lit.:* Pignatti, 1968,
p. 123, pl. 357.
No paintings are known which can be closely
related to these sketches. Probably they are
studies for that series of family portraits,
such as the Albrizzi Family in the Rubin de
Cervin Albrizzi collection, Venice (Pignatti,
1968, pl. 218), which Longhi executed during
the 1760s and 1770s.

Pietro Longhi
64. *Dancer and Sketch of a Female Head*
Inv. no. 485.
Black chalk, heightened with white, on grey paper; 268 x 333 mm.
Prov.: Correr, 1830. *Lit.:* Pignatti, 1968, p. 122, pl. 339; Idem, 1983, p. 125, pl. 76.
Exhibitions: Bruxelles, 1983, no. 76.
This figure of a dancing girl recalls, particularly in the position of her legs and the pointed foot, the various versions of the painting entitled *La Furlana* (a Friuli folkdance), such as the ones in the Ca' Rezzonico (Pignatti, 1968, p. 99, pl. 92) and in the Querini Stampalia (Idem, 1968, p. 111, pl. 94), and *The Dancer* in the Crespi collection, Milan (Idem, 1968, p. 90, pl. 104). The figure in the drawing is, however, in reverse to the painting; her arms are outstretched and she seems to have castanets in her hands, while in the paintings the girls' arms are lowered so as to lift their skirts a little. The girl in the drawing is also wearing an odd hat which gives her head a somewhat curious aspect.

The female head on the right side of the sheet is very sketchy, except for the detail of the ribbon which adorns her delicate neck, creating a charming colour effect.

The drawing probably dates from the 1760s.

Pietro Longhi
65. *Shooting in the Lagoon*
Inv. no. 475.
Black chalk, heightened with white, on brown paper; 292 x 450 mm.
Inscr.: 'La camisiola qui; I zocheti' (in the artist's hand).
Prov.: Correr, 1830. *Lit.:* Ravà, 1923, p. 133; Valcanover, 1956, p. 25; 'La peinture italienne', 1960, no. 338; Pignatti, 1963, no. 54; Idem, 1964, no. 54; Idem, 1965, no. 60.
Exhibitions: Paris, 1960, no. 338; Washington, 1963, no. 54; Venice, 1964, no. 54; London, 1965, no. 60.
Most probably sketched on the spot, this drawing is a study for the painting now in the Galleria Querini Stampalia, Venice, and it is dated around 1770 by Valcanover. At this time Longhi's style is marked by a tendency towards freer lines and more summary forms, but the drawings retain their practical function as steps in his working process. The inscriptions, notes on the white shirts of the boatmen and details of the boat, are additional aids to the artist's memory.

Pietro Longhi
66. *The Bird Cage*
Inv. no. 535.
Black chalk, heightened with white, on brown paper; 290 x 430 mm.
Inscr.: 'il Grugnetto oscuro / la machia sin soto il colo Giala / rosso a torno a lochio e tuto / il Corpo verdolin / qualche peneta roseta su / zalla abasso / Lochio rosetto e la pupilla nera / (in the artist's hand).
Prov.: Correr, 1830. *Lit.:* Moschini, 1956, fig. 11; Pignatti, 1965, no. 58.
Exhibitions: Rotterdam, 1964, no. 56; London, 1965, no. 58.
This witty drawing is related to a second one in the Correr (no. 447), which is preparatory for a lost painting, *The Music Lesson*. The inscription, in Venetian dialect, gives colour notes with surprising, and at the same time poetic, precision.

1946 *(op. cit.)*; this covered only the eighty-seven larger sheets. On the last page of the original sketchbook an authentic inscription gives the names of G.B. and Domenico Tiepolo and the price of the volume in 1770 – eight *sequins*, which Byam Shaw (1962, p. 22) calculates to be worth about twelve dollars – and states that the drawings were 'presi dal naturale' i.e., from models and not after frescoes. This inscription is evidence that the sketchbook contains drawings by both Giambattista and Giandomenico; scholars have long endeavoured to differentiate between them. In his book on Giandomenico's drawings, Byam Shaw gives a masterly summary of the results of this research. Some new discoveries have now allowed us to proceed further and to distinguish the style of Giambattista from his sons'.

The present drawing is a study for the portrait of Antonio Bossi included in the Würzburg staircase fresco by Gian Battista. The substantial differences in the legs and drapery, as well as the detail of the sitter's head at the upper right of the drawing, and proofs that it was made for and not after the fresco, and, consequently, is by Gian Battista.

Gian Battista Tiepolo (1696-1770)
67. *Four Female Nudes*
Inv. no. 203.
Black pencil, pen and sepia, with sepia wash, heightened with white; 220 x 185 mm.
Inscr.: 'Tiepolo:io' (in the artist's hand); 'G.B. Tiepolo' (in an eighteenth-century hand).
Prov.: Correr, 1830. *Lit.:* Pignatti, 1963, no. 104; Byam Shaw, 1964, p. 179; Pignatti, 1964, no. 104; Idem, 1965, no. 103.
Exhibitions: Washington, 1963, no. 104; Venice, 1964, no. 104; London, 1965, no. 103.
A fine drawing, probably a study for a fountain or a balustrade sculpture such as appears, for instance, in the *Death of Hyacinth* in the Thyssen collection (*c.* 1753). The drawing is closely related in style to the Birtschansky *Nymphs*, which also bears an eighteenth-century inscription similar to the one seen here (Cailleux, 1952, p. 41, pl. 3).

Gian Battista Tiepolo
68. *Study of a Standing Gentleman*
Inv. no. 7074.
Red chalk, heightened with white, on blue-grey paper; 445 x 285 mm.
Prov.: Gatteri, 1885. *Lit.:* Lorenzetti, 1946, p. 10, no. 16 verso; Pignatti, 1963, no. 98; Idem, 1964, no. 98; Idem, 1965, no. 100.
Exhibitions: Washington, 1963, no. 98; Venice, 1964, no. 98; London, 1965, no. 100.
Giovanni Battista Tiepolo worked in the Würzburg Residenz from October 1750 to November 1753, with the assistance of his sons Giovanni Domenico and Lorenzo, and the Italian stucco decorator Antonio Bossi. A sketchbook of eighty-seven pages, to which nearly 230 smaller drawings connected with the frescos at Würzburg had been added, came to the Correr from the painter Lorenzo Gatteri. After it had been broken up, Lorenzetti re-established part of it in its original order and published a facsimile edition in

Gian Battista Tiepolo
69. *Sketch of a Female Head and Two Unfinished Similar Sketches*
Inv. no. 7141.
Black pencil, heightened with white; 445 x 285 mm.
Prov.: Gatteri, 1885. *Lit.:* Lorenzetti, 1946, no. 83 verso; Vigni, 1956, pp. 363-5; Lamb and Von Freeden, 1956, fig. 90; Byam Shaw, 1962, no. 22.
This is another sheet from the Gatteri sketchbook and it is certainly a study for the America fresco at Würzburg. The face is in fact very close to that of the girl carrying a basket on top of her head, who appears on the right section of the fresco.

99

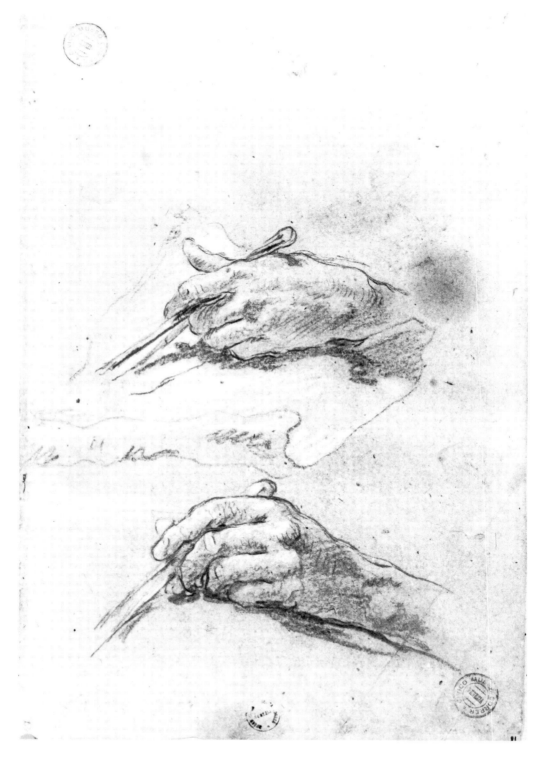

Gian Domenico Tiepolo (1727-1804)
70. *Study of Hands*
Inv. no. 7063.
Red chalk, heightened with white, on blue-grey paper; 445 x 290 mm.
Prov.: Gatteri, 1885. *Lit.:* Lorenzetti, 1946, p. 9, no. 5; Pignatti, 1963, no. 109; Idem, 1964, no. 110; Idem, 1965, no. 107.
Exhibitions: Washington, 1963, no. 109; Venice, 1964, no. 110; London, 1965, no. 107.
This is one of the few large Gatteri sketches which can surely be given to Giandomenico. It must be one of those drawings 'presi dal naturale', to which the original inscription on the last page of the sketchbook refers. In fact, it has the appearance of a drawing made at the mirror, and there is no mention of Giandomenico having been left-handed. In the large collection of Urlaub drawings at Würzburg there is one of exactly the same subject, with only slight variations. This leads us to speculate whether there was a 'study hour' for the whole Tiepolo circle in the Würzburg atelier.

Giambattista Tiepolo
71. *Study of a Slave*
Inv. no. 7157.
Red chalk, heightened with white, on blue paper; 275 x 305 mm.
Prov.: Gatteri, 1885. *Lit.:* Pignatti, 1965, no. 102; Idem, 1966, p. 893.
Exhibitions: London, 1965, no. 102.
Another revealing sheet from the Gatteri sketchbook, useful in distinguishing the graphic style of Giambattista from that of Giandomenico. The drawing is connected with the slave in the left portion of the Africa fresco at Würzburg. A typical record of the fresco was made by Giandomenico, in a drawing room now at Stuttgart (no. 1473; Hadeln, 1927, pl. 140). Its technique is the same as that of the drawing shown here, and the media and the paper are almost identical. But no one would dare to suggest that the style could be in doubt: the tremulous, slender, reworked line of the Giandomenico drawing at Stuttgart is very far from the fluid, structural, creative style of the present work, which cannot be by anyone other than Giambattista. Further confirmation can be found in the close stylistic resemblance between the present drawing and the *Study of a man with a pipe*, also in the Correr (inv. no. 7070). Moreover, the figure in no. 71 varies considerably from the slave in the fresco, both in the anatomy (where the muscles are 'realized', and not merely copied), and in the drapery; and also in the different position of the head, which is determined by the weight of the sacks that the figure is lowering. On this evidence we may safely conclude that the younger Tiepolos followed the inventions of Giambattista, but that Giambattista himself often made changes in the process of work in the frescoes. The subsequent drawings after the fresco were usually made by Domenico, or occasionally by Lorenzo or by the German assistants (Urlaub, for instance, whose sketchbooks, still attributed in some of the literature to Tiepolo, are at Würzburg University). These records, or true 'copies', are always strictly identical with the frescoes.

Marco Ricci (1676-1729)
72. Landscape with Peasants and a Mill
Inv. no. 8220.
Pen and sepia; 220 x 238 mm.
Prov.: Brass, 1964. *Lit.:* Pilo, 1961, p. 172, and 1963, no. 104; Valcanover, 1964, no. 76; Pignatti, 1965, no. 66.
Exhibitions: London, 1965, no. 66.
A brilliant sketch which illustrates Ricci's Titianesque manner, probably after 1720. The open expanse of landscape, bathed in soft light akin to that in some of Ricci's later paintings, suggests to me that Professor Blunt (1957, p. 39) is right in describing such drawings – which are in the style of Windsor nos. 84 and 98 – as later works.

Francesco Simonini (1686-1753)
73. *Cavalry Battle*
Inv. no. 1763.
Pen and sepia, and sepia wash;
213 x 275 mm.
Prov.: Gamba. *Lit.:* Delogu, 1930-1, p. 840.
Simonini was born in Parma, where he was
trained by the painter Spolverini, and came
to Venice after a short stay in Florence,
where he studied the works of Bergognone.
The many drawings by Simonini at the
Correr show his interest in battle scenes,
interest which he shared with Giuseppe
Zais, for many paintings and drawings of
similar subjects by Zais are known.

The technique of this drawing is quite
sketchy, with dense and dramatic brushwork and nervous pen strokes which create
an overall movement across the surface.
This small sheet is either ignored or
mentioned with a different inventory number
by Delogu in his article on Simonini's
drawings in Venice (Dedalo, 1930-1, pp. 827-
40).

Giuseppe Zais (1709-84)
74. *Landscape with Women Washing*
Inv. no. 5769.
Brush and sepia wash and tempera;
400 x 540 mm.
Prov.: Molin, 1813. *Lit.:* Delogu, 1930,
p. 142; Pignatti, 1956, p. 182; Idem, 1963,
no. 66; Idem, 1964, no. 66.
Exhibitions: Washington, 1963, no. 66;
Venice, 1964, no. 66.

Giuseppe Zais
75. *Landscape with a Woman Selling Eggs*
Inv. no. 5770
Brush and sepia wash, and tempera;
400 x 540 mm.
Prov.: Molin, 1813. *Lit.:* Delogu, 1930,
p. 142; Pignatti, 1956, p. 182; Idem, 1965,
no. 72.
Exhibitions: London, 1965, no. 72.
Another of four large tempera drawings in
the Correr, in Zais's most charming manner,
this was also intended for sale to collectors.
Such drawings in colour were probably
executed after the 1750s, and they show
evident contacts with Zuccarelli, notably in
the light shading and brightness of colour.
The crisp, fluent use of outline; influenced by
Marco Ricci, shows the difference between
the two artists.

of the figures and the stressed graphicism (Rizzi, 1967, 101). Pignatti, on the other hand, proposes a dating around the 1730s, noting in the drawing a vague Canalettesque inspiration, which is typical of the last period of Carlevaris's activity (1966, 196).

Most probably these drawings were made by Luca in a short period of time, as studies to be used for later paintings. As the earliest picture in which it is possible to identify the boats of the Correr album is the *Sea Port with a Tower* at Windsor, dating from immediately before 1714, the whole series of drawings might be dated around the beginning of the 1720s.

The present drawing is very different in technique from the others included in the album. The pencil lines reinforced with pen and brown ink, the shaded areas underlined with a dense pen hatching and the little wash shading are unique among the album sheets. Even the setting of the two boats in the lagoon, with an island with a high tower (perhaps Burano) on the left and distant hills on the right, does not appear in any of the other drawings. Though related to the subject of the boat studies, this drawing, almost foretelling Canaletto's manner, presents such a finish that it is supposed to be executed for sale to some collector.

Francesco Zuccarelli (1702-1788)
76. *Landscape with Peasants*
Inv. no. 5379.
Pen and sepia, brush and sepia wash, and coloured washes, on yellowish paper; 220 x 360 mm.
Prov.: Molin, 1813. *Lit.:* Pignatti, 1956, p. 178; Idem, 1963, no. 68; Idem, 1964, no. 68; Idem, 1965, no. 73.
Exhibitions: Washington, 1963, no. 68; Venice, 1964, no. 68; London, 1965, no. 73. Although at the outset Zuccarelli did not appear to have the makings of a great draughtsman, he has left a large number of excellent drawings. From pencil or pen studies to large album-sheets, his drawings always show a genuine painterly quality which brings them close in style to his paintings. The present drawing has been badly cut at the edges, but we can still admire the immediacy of his colour effects, which have been achieved with characteristic washes over the penwork. I would suggest a date around the 1750s, because of similarities to drawings in the Tassi album (Bassi-Rathgeb, 1948).

Luca Carlevaris (1663-1730)
77. *Lagoon with Two Boats*
Inv. no. 5949.
Pencil, pen and brown ink and sepia wash, heightened with white; grey-blue paper on supporting sheet; 200 x 199 mm.
Inscr.: 'Luca Carlevaris', '13' (in a nineteenth-century hand).
Prov.: Corniani Algarotti, 1893. *Lit.:* Nebbia, 1931, 312; Mauroner, 1931, 25; Idem, 1944, 67; Idem, 1945, 69; Rizzi, 1964, 63; Idem, 1967, 101; Pignatti, 1963, 46; Idem, 1964, 54; Idem, 1966, 196; Idem, 1967, 252; Idem, 1970, 91; Bonicatti, 1964, 137; Pignatti, 1980, no. 79.
Exhibitions: Washington, 1964, no. 71.
This drawing is included in an album of 24 pages inscribed (in a nineteenth-century hand) as having belonged to Count Corniani Algarotti of Venice. The album was acquired by the Correr in 1893 and the drawings show various types of boats. Their dating is still controversial. Rizzi suggests that they belong to Carlevaris's early activity, probably to the period after his return from Rome and before the publication of *Le fabriche e vedute* in 1703, and justifies his opinion by pointing out the subject matter's objectivity, reminiscent of the Netherlandish painters, the awkwardness

Luca Carlevaris
78. *Man-of-War Lying at Anchor*
Inv. no. 5959.
Pencil, pen and brown ink, and sepia wash, heightened with white; Havana brown paper on supporting sheet; 275 x 209 mm.
Inscr. 'Luca Carlevaris, 23' (in an eighteenth-century hand).
Prov.: Corniani Algarotti, 1893. *Lit.:* same as previous.
This man-of-war lying at anchor appears in the centre of the painting *Harbour with Roman Monument and Arch* now in the Sacerdoti Gallery, Milan, dated 1714 (repr. in Rizzi, 1967, no. 78). The only difference is that the sail is not placed in such a way as to protect the ship's deck from the sun's rays.

In the drawing the top part of the high masting, which goes beyond the sheet's upper edge, is transferred to the upper right corner of the same sheet.

23.

Canaletto (Antonio Canal called)
(1697-1768)
80. *Four Architectural Sketches*
Inv. no. 1785.
Pen and sepia; white paper on supporting
sheet; 232 x 170 mm.
Inscr.: 'Canaletto' (in a nineteenth-century
hand); 'per la Cademia' (in the artist's
hand).
Prov.: Gamba, 1841. *Lit.:* Muraro, 1953, 49;
Pignatti, 1960, 34; Idem, 1963, no. 72; Idem,
1964, no. 72; Idem, 1965, no. 76; Idem, 1965,
no. 95; Idem, 1973, no. 66; Constable, 1962,
no. 626; Idem, 1976, no. 626; Pignatti, 1980,
no. 57.
Exhibitions: Washington, 1963, no. 72;
Venice, 1964, no. 72; London, 1965, no. 76.
This sheet was first mentioned by Muraro,
who dated it around 1720 (1953, p. 49). Later
it was related by Pignatti to the painting
(now in the Gallerie dell'Accademia) that
Canaletto presented to the Venetian Academy
after his election on September 11, 1763.
This is confirmed by the inscription menti-
oning the Accademia. Showing also the inner
courtyard of a fourteenth-century Venetian
building no longer in existence, the sheet is
typical of the artist's 'documentary style',
with brilliant effects of light on the sunny
façade. The outside staircase is reminiscent
of those in the Campiello della Fenice and
the Campiello del Renier, near the Rialto.

Luca Carlevaris
79. *Pedlars and Musicians*
Inv. no. 6954.
Pencil and pen and brown ink;
282 x 200 mm.
Inscr.: '17' (red pencil).
Prov.: Mauroner bequest, 1948. *Lit.:*
Mauroner, 1931, 25; Idem, 1945, 70; Rizzi,
1963, 91; Idem, 1967, 102; Valcanover, 1964,
24; Pignatti, 1980, no. 95.
Exhibitions: Udine-Roma, 1963-64, no. 72;
Groningen-Rotterdam, 1964, no. 24.
These figures drawn from life in the *calli*
(streets) and *campi* (squares) of Venice were
probably sketches to be used for paintings.

The figures of the water-seller in the centre
of the top part of the sheet is squared up, in
order to be transferred on canvas.

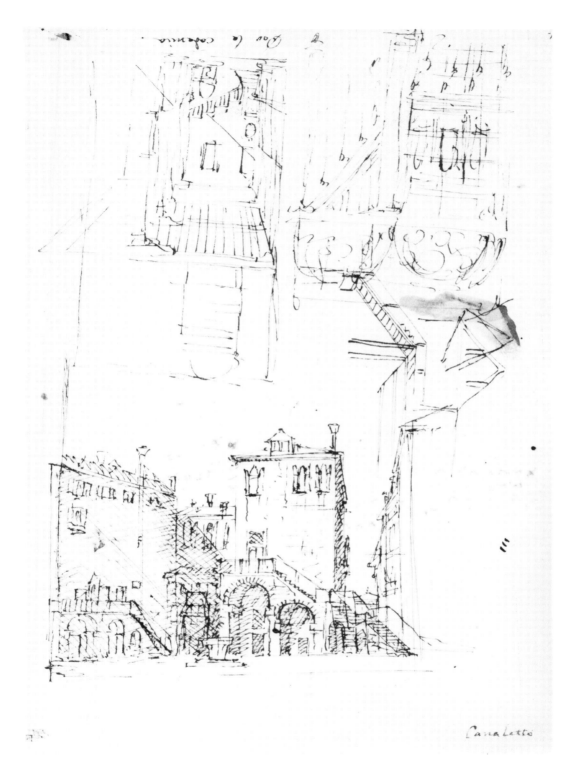

Bernardo Bellotto (1720-1780)
81. *Country Landscape with Peasants*
Black pencil and pen and sepia;
278 x 305 mm.
Prov.: Frigerio collection; Antonio Morassi
collection, Milan (loan 1983). *Lit.:* Pignatti,
1963, no. 73.
Exhibitions: Washington, 1963, no. 73.
Bellotto's drawings are generally carefully
drawn and rather stiff; rarely do they attain
the vibrancy of Canaletto, as does this
landscape, which shows a country church
surrounded by houses with figures in the
foreground. Characteristic wavy lines, in a
style similar to the *View of Padua* in the
Koenigs collection (Fritzsche, p. 137, fig. 15),
confirm an attribution to Bellotto.

Tommaso Temanza (1705-1789)
82. *Chiesa di S. Maria Maddalena*
Inv. no. 6109.
Pen and brush, Indian ink and grey wash;
391 x 181 mm.
Inscr.: above left: 'D'
Prov.: Wcowich-Lazzari, 1896. *Lit.:* Moschini,
1806; Temanza, 1811; Moschini, 1815;
Cicognara-Diedo-Selva, 1815-20; Negri,
1820; Cicognara, 1824-53; Gamba, 1842; de
Tipaldo, 1844; Selvatico, 1847; Temanza
(Lettere), 1858; Ivanoff, 1959; Bassi, 1962;
Temanza, 1963; Haskell, 1966; Brusatin,
1969 and 1980; Olivato, 1970-73 and 1975;
Romanelli, 1977 and 1978.
This is the design for the little church of
S. Maria Maddalena. The church is not only

an architectural masterpiece in Venice, but one of the cornerstones of Neoclassical architecture. The Church of the Maddalena was designed in 1760 and building began in 1763, but it had not been completely finished by Temanza's death in 1789, although the major outlines were already completed by 1778.

Temanza himself summed up the programmatic character of the building in a letter to F.M. Preti: 'Simple and regular. The outside corresponds to the inside and the proportions are musical.'

In fact, the question of 'proportion' is only one of the architectural problems brought together in an exemplary fashion by a building like the Maddalena. The first is that of the classical and Palladian models to which the architect intended to make reference; the second, that of the congruity and linguistic correctness in his choice of orders (significantly, and in Alberti's style, Temanza adopts the Ionic order, since the building was dedicated to the veneration of a female saint); and the last is that of the difficulty of inserting a building into a delicate and most individual environment like that of Venice.

However, Temanza manages to resolve every one of the questions that faced him with great self-confidence: not only does the Maddalena fit happily into the bend of the canal, isolated but cleverly linked with the texture of buildings and the urban function of the context. As a result, the building also becomes the manifesto of the new style in Venetian architecture, bringing together many innovations taken from the work of contemporary or earlier architects in its forms and its allusive message: it unites the functionalism of the eighteenth century with the Roman and Classical styles of Palladianism, the mathematical 'scientism' of the French and Italian rationalists, and an absoluteness and simplicity of pure form.

One needs only to refer briefly to the Maddalena's critical success: after encountering an initial difficulty with the critics, which can be blamed on an excessive secularity in the conception of a religious building, the Maddalena became a necessary point of reference for the next generation of architects, who explicitly set it up as the cornerstone of a new age in Venetian architecture. It is enough to point to the evidence of Selva or to the illustrative catalogue compiled by Diedo for the *Fabbriche di Venezia*. Thanks to Selva, Lazzari and Diedo himself, the building stands at the head of the whole series of academic exercises on the theme of a construction on a circular plan.

Most of Tommaso Temanza's architectural drawings are kept in the collections of the Biblioteca del Seminario Patriarcale.

The Correr Museum owns a small group of plans, besides those of the Maddalena, which concern the *casino* of Zenobio dei Carmini, a theatre, some hydraulic engineering works for river sluices, and other projects. Temanza is a very dry, almost harsh and ungraceful draughtsman: he cares nothing for late-Baroque decoration in working out graphic elaboration, and does not share the Neoclassical designers' delight in illustration (and they often tended to be more illustrators than architects), as if to show his superiority and even his irritation when faced with the apparatus of the art of building, as opposed to the importance of conceptual choices and the qualifying capacity of justifying linguistic options.

Giambattista Piranesi (?) (Mogliano, Venice
1720 – Rome 1778)
83. *Interior of a Portico with a Hanging Staircase*
Inv. no. 8405.
Pen and wash, sepia and brown ink on
yellowish paper mounted on card with pencil
embellishment; 214 x 133 mm.
Prov.:, Musatti, 1967. *Lit.:* Pignatti 1970,
nos. 3-4; Idem, 1971, nos. 1-2; Bettagno,
1978.
The attribution of this little drawing from
the Musatti collection now in the Correr was
suggested by Pignatti in the *Catalogue* of
1970. Many elements, not least of which is
the nervous discontinuity of line, support
this hypothesis. The scenographically accen-
tuated formulation and the perspective
complexity of the view suggest a dating of
around 1750, by analogy with Bettagno's
proposal for a group of London architectural fantasies (c.f. Bettagno, 1978, nos. 16-
29), namely those in the Shatzki Collection
in New York or in the Kunsthalle in
Hamburg, no. 1915 (Pignatti).

Even though traces remain of the themes
of the architectural caprices of the landscape tradition, we should also notice the
magniloquent and visionary emphasis of the
composition that is typical of the author of
the *Carceri*.

Gaetano Zompini (1700-1778)
84. *Il Codega (The Linkboy)*
Inv. no. 232.
Pen and black ink; 190 x 140 mm.
Prov.: Soranzo, 1865. *Lit.:* L. Moretti, 1968.
This is one of the 95 preparatory drawings
executed by Zompini for a collection of
engravings which he published in Venice
between 1753 and 1754. All the drawings are
now owned by the Correr and all, except one
(no. 59), depict subjects appearing in the
engravings. The title of the collection is *Le
arti che vanno per via nella città di Venezia* (The
strolling arts in the city of Venice); it includes
60 engravings, 40 of which appeared in the
first edition of 1753, while the other 20 were
published about a year later.

Under each engraving there are some lines
in Venetian dialect which illustrate the Art
depicted above.

The present drawing is the final preparatory study of the art of the 'Codega', the man
who lit the Venetians their way at night.

There are two other rapid sketches of this
scene in the Correr, certainly drawn from
life, in pencil and then reinforced with the
pen. This drawing, unlike most of the other
ones, is not in reverse to the engraving.

Pier Antonio Novellie (1729-1804)
85. *Apollo with the Poets*
Inv. no. 3661.
Red pencil, pen and black ink, and grey wash; 240 x 169 mm.
Prov.: Correr, 1830. *Lit.:* Pignatti, 1963, no. 114; Idem, 1964, no. 114; Idem, 1965, no. 115.
Exhibitions: Washington, 1963, no. 114; Venice, 1964, no. 114; London, 1965, no. 115.
A fine drawing, showing the artist's best 'finished style', probably made for a title page or book illustration. The subject – five poets and a poetess paying homage to Apollo – is unique. The origins of Novelli's drawing style – and of his painting as well – can be traced back to the Pellegrini-Diziani school. There is also some influence of Fontebasso in his shading, but the main characteristic of his style is probably his interest in Rembrandt. Novelli's son Francesco later reproduced heads by Rembrandt in a famous edition of prints.

Large collections of Novelli's drawings are now in the Correr, Albertina, Cooper Union, Princeton University, Detroit Museums and in the Scholz collection.

Bartolomeo Tarsia (1711-1765)
86. *Triumph of the Olympian Gods*
Inv. no. 246.
Black pencil, pen and sepia, and tempera on
yellowish paper; 270 x 410 mm.
Prov.: Correr, 1830. *Lit.:* Pignatti, 1963,
no. 30; Byam Shaw, 1964, p. 178; Salmina,
1964, no. 77; Pignatti, 1964, no. 30; Idem,
1965, no. 36.
This is one of the four *modelletti* in the Correr
Museum, attributed to Tarsia on the basis of
evidence in the old inventories. Dr Salamina
kindly informed me that they were made in
1750 for the frescoes at Petershof, Leningrad. Tarsia has the qualities of a draughtsman close to Diziani, specifically in the use of
luminous washes. Byam Shaw mentions a
fine sheet from the same hand, dated 1745,
now in the possession of Mr Francis Watson,
London.

Francesco Zugno (1709-1787)
87. *The Holy Family and S. Filippo Neri*
Inv. no. 1300.
Black pencil, 355 x 185 mm.
Inscr.: 'Tiepolo' (in an eighteenth-century
hand).
Prov.: Correr, 1830. *Lit.:* Pignatti, 1965,
no. 114.
Exhibitions: London, 1965, no. 114.
This drawing illustrates the most characteristic manner of Zugno: his timid, meticulous
style shows more awareness of the illustrative traditions of Piazzetta than of Tiepolo.
The drawing closely corresponds in style to
certain paintings, such as the charming
altarpiece at the Ca 'Rezzonico (Pignatti,
1960, p. 400).
   A drawing of this type, with an eighteenth-
century inscription, 'Zugno dis', is owned by
the Metropolitan Museum, New York, and
another by the Witt collection, Courtauld
Institute.

Gian Domenico Tiepolo (1727-1804)
89. *The Ballad Singers*
Inv. no. 6042.
Black pencil, pen and sepia, and sepia wash;
375 x 505 mm.
Inscr.: 'Dom. Tiepolo f. 1791' (in the artist's
hand).
Prov.: Cantalamessa. *Lit.:* Pignatti, 1951,
p. 196; no. 128; Idem, 1963, no. 112; Idem,
1964, no. 109; Idem, 1965, no. 112.
Exhibitions: Venice, 1951, no. 128; Washington, 1963, no. 112; Venice, 1964, no. 109;
London, 1965, no. 112.
This is one of the best of Giandomenico's
drawings of contemporary scenes, most of
which were executed in the 1790s. Byam
Shaw states that no less than twenty of these
works bear, like this one, the date 1791 (1962,
p. 47). The artist no doubt intended these
drawings to be grotesque and satirical. They
were probably inspired by his father's
caricatures, of which he made free copies,
but they are more ambitious to scale. These
sheets are generally of a large size (approximately 12 x 16 in.), and enclosed by a ruled
margin, and they possess the quality of
finished pictorial compositions. Some of the
most significant drawings are in the Talleyrand collection, in the museums of Boston,
Minneapolis, Cleveland, and Hartford, and
in private collections, particularly in France
(Byam Shaw, 1962, nos. 59-77). Giandomenico's Punchinello series – over a
hundred drawings, now widely dispersed –
was probably also done in the 1790s. The
actual subject of *The Ballad Singers* remains
uncertain, but it probably signifies more
than a grotesque double serenade for two
voices and quartet. The subject is probably a
street-musicians' performance in some
imagined Venetian square.

Michelangelo Schiavone
88. *Adoration of the Magi*
Inv. no. 20.
Pen and brown ink and wash, heightened
with white; 580 x 420 mm.
Inscr.: 'Tiepolo fece'.
Lit.: unpublished..
This drawing corresponds in reverse to the
famous engraving of the *Adoration of the Magi*
by G.B. Tiepolo (D.V.I.).
   Knox mentions two other similar drawings,
one at Epinal (1952, no. 14, pl. 10) and
another in the Fogg Museum, New York
(1970, no. 22), both attributed to him by the
painter Raggi. We are more inclined, however, towards an attribution to Michelangelo
Schiavone, an artist from Chioggia.

Francesco Guardi (1712-1793)
90. *Madonna*
Inv. no. 6949.
Black chalk heightened with white; brown
paper on cardboard; 340 x 246 mm.
Prov.: unknown or Correr, 1830. *Lit.:*
Muraro, 1949, 125; Pignatti, 1963, 245;
Idem, 1963, no. 74; Idem, 1964, no. 74; Idem,
1965, no. 77; Idem, 1967, XIX; Morassi, 102,
no. 129; Binion, 1976, 275; Pignatti, 1983,
no. 514.
Exhibitions: Washington, 1963; Venice, 1964;
London, 1965.
This inspired Madonna belongs most
probably to Francesco's early activity, when
the younger of the two brothers is still
influenced by Gian Antonio. A dating around
the beginning of the 1760s is confirmed by its
connection with the paintings, always better
datable than the drawings. This is the preparatory sketch for the Haberstock Madonna,
Berlin, not for, as it has always been believed,
the Tecchio Madonna, whose preparatory
drawing is in the Zwicky collection,
Arlesheim (Byam Shaw, 1962, 50, no. 56), or
for the Madonna in the Padua Museum
(Morassi, 1973, cat. 188, 187, 189). The
Haberstock Madonna appears to be a very
early work and is therefore reminiscent of
Antonio's style, particularly in the light
colour nuances. In this drawing, however,
the characteristic jagged drapery and sharp
highlights differ from Gian Antonio's style,
which is noticeably lighter.

Francesco Guardi
91. *Saint Niccolo', Saint Joseph and the Infant Christ and Other Figure Sketches*
Inv. no. 1221.
Pen and brown ink; 174 x 148 mm.

Prov.: Correr, 1830. *Lit.:* Fiocco, 1923, 28, 29, 67, no. 23; Lorenzetti, 1936, no. 84; Pallucchini, 1943, 38, no. 14; Ragghianti, 1953, 22; Moschini, 1956, fig. 54; Pignatti, 1965, 26, no. 82; Idem, 1967, fig. XLIV; Morassi, 1975, 123-124, no. 263; Binion, 1976, 308; Pignatti, 1983, no. 533.
Exhibitions: Venice, 1936; London, 1965.
This drawing was first related by Fiocco to the Vigo altarpiece (for Saint Niccolò) and to

the Toledo altarpiece (for Saint Joseph), on the basis of mere iconographic similarities (Morassi, 1973, cat. 58, 46). Pallucchini, on the other hand, connects it with two other drawings also depicting Saint Niccolò (nos. 532, 533) that he considers as preparatory studies for the Miramare banner (Morassi, 1973, cat. 53). Those drawings, however, are too different from the painting to accept Pallucchini's identification and dating around 1760-65 without reserve. We cannot neglect the clear similarity of Saint Joseph with later drawings such as the Saint Mark in Count Seilern's collection (Morassi, 1975, cat. 152). Also the *macchiette* (stylized figure sketches) with the large feathered hats, are typical of Francesco's late period, around 1780.

Francesco Guardi
92. *The Corte del Ridotto*
Inv. no. 705.
Black pencil, pen and sepia, and sepia wash; yellowish paper on cardboard; 166 x 220 mm.
Inscr.: 'Corte del Ridotto a San Moisè' (in the hand of Nicolò Barozzi).
Prov.: Correr, 1830.
Lit.: Fiocco, 1923, 72, no. 82; Il Settecento Italiano, 1932, fig. 196; Lorenzetti, 1936, no. 50; Pallucchini, 1943, no. 48; Idem, 1947, no. 179; Schönheit des XVIII Jahr., 1955, no. 147; Italian Drawings, 1960-61, 67, no. 137; Venetiaanse Tekeningen, 1964, 28, no. 33; Pignatti, 1965, 26, no. 84; Idem, 1967, XXX; Idem, 1970, fig. at p. 9; Morassi, 1975, 113, no. 198; Pignatti, 1983, no. 560.
Exhibitions: Venice, 1929; Venice, 1936; Lausanne, 1947; Zurich, 1955; Washington, 1960-61; Groningen, 1964; London, 1965.
The inscription, in the hand of the former Director of the Correr Museum, certainly refers, as in many other cases, to an inscrip-

tion on the back of the original mounting paper. The identification of the setting must therefore be accurate. The present drawing is datable before 1768, for it shows the Ridotto before Maccaruzzi's restorations were carried out in that year. Pallucchini identified a later drawing, showing the same view after the restorations, in the Musée Bonnat, Bayonne (Morassi, 1975, cat. 199); other similar drawings were acquired by the Anderson Gallery, New York, in 1921.

The Ridotto, a famous gambling house, was closed by the Republic in 1774, to prevent Venetian nobles from squandering their estates.

Francesco's style is here fully developed and it can be compared to that of the twelve *Ducal Festivities* (Morassi, 1973, cat. 243-254), painted around that time. The *macchietta* shows by now its typical character, creating a sort of foreground, for the play of Guardi's luminiscent glazes.

130

Francesco Guardi
93. *Landscape with Country House and Porch*
Inv. no. 689.
Pen and sepia; yellowish paper on cardboard;
214 x 175 mm.
Prov.: Correr, 1830. *Lit.:* Lorenzetti, 1936,
no. 130; Pallucchini, 1943, 56, no. 130;
Goering, 1944, 58, 83; De Maffei, 1951, 23,
42; Schönheit des XVIII Jahr, 1955, no. 148;
Pignatti, 1963, 50, no. 83; Idem, 1964, 61,
no. 83; Idem, 1965, 26-7, no. 86; Idem, 1967,
XXXVII; Zampetti, 1967, 354, no. 160;
Morassi, 1975, 181, no. 592; Pignatti, 1983,
no. 588.
Exhibitions: Venice, 1936; Zurich, 1955;
Washington, 1963; Venice, 1964; London,
1965; Venice, 1967.
This drawing has been rightly connected
with the view of Castel Cogolo *On the Way to
Trento*, and dated around the time when
Francesco Guardi made a visit to his native
country, Val di Sole, in 1778 (De Maffei,
1951, 23). I cannot accept, however, the old
identification of this subject as the Guardi
house at Mastellina, near Trento (Simonson,
1904, 24). A direct comparison will show that
the ancient home of the Guardi family has
two main storeys instead of the one in the
drawing; moreover, it has no balconies and it
still retains a small but pretentious doorway
leading to the lower hall, which is closed at
the back, unlike the rustic portico which
appears here. Morassi mentions a painting in
the Speelman collection, London (1973,
cat. 852) and a copy by Giacomo Guardi in a
Swiss collection (*ibid.*, fig. 647). Francesco's
style is here very effective, by means of
vibrant lines and a sparse hatching, creating
rich pictorial effects.

Francesco Guardi
94. *View with Ruins, Boats and Fishermen*
Inv. no. 7318.
Pen and sepia, heightened with white; blue-
grey prepared paper; 306 x 280 mm.
Prov.: Correr, 1830 (?). *Lit.:* Brunetti, 1926,
pl. LXXXIII; Lorenzetti, 1936, no. 61;
Pallucchini, 1943, 58, no. 152; Arslan, 1944,
8 (imitator); Moschini, 1956, fig. 130;
Morassi, 1975, 164, no. 487; Pignatti, 1983,
no. 603.
Exhibitions: Venice, 1936.
This large caprice view should be related to
the similar painting in the Poldi Pezzoli
Museum, Milan (Morassi, 1973, cat. 713).
Pallucchini mentions another caprice view
which can be connected with this drawing
and is in the De Szeth Giovio collection at
Alzate; the painting, together with other
caprice views, was bought by Count
Rezzonico directly from Francesco at a price
of one *scute*.

EIGHTEENTH CENTURY

Francesco Guardi
95. *The Visit*
Inv. no. 897.
Pen and sepia; yellowish paper (reinforcement on the doorway of the palace); 129 x 174 mm.
Inscr.: Fragment of a letter addressed to the Litta family at Caprarola (in an eighteenth-century hand, on the verso).
Prov.: Correr, 1830. *Lit.:* Il Settecento Italiano, 1932, fig. 183; Lorenzetti, 1936, no. 3; Pallucchini, 1943, 43, nos. 47a, 47b; Goering, 1944, 48, 82, no. 89; Byam Shaw, 1951, 67, no. 47; Ragghianti, 1953, 19, 25, no. 43; Moschini, 1956, fig. 99; Parker–Byam Shaw, 1962, 65, no. 88; Kostens Venedig, 1962, 233-4, no. 310; Pignatti, 1963, 49, no. 80; Bonicatti, 1964, 140; Pignatti, 1964, 56-7, no. 80; Fiocco, 1965, fig. 51; Pignatti, 1965, 26, no. 85; Idem, 1967, LII; Morassi, 1975, no. 221; Pignatti, 1983, no. 654.
Exhibitions: Venice, 1929; Venice, 1936; Stockholm, 1962; Washington, 1963; Venice, 1964; London, 1965.
This subject, the reception of a visitor at a palace entrance, was depicted several times by Francesco Guardi: there is a simplified

version in the Correr (no. 673, probably a copy by Giacomo Guardi), another sketch is in the Cooper Union Museum, New York (Pallucchini, 1943, no. 47) and there is a painting in the Frick collection which allowed Byam Shaw to identify the place as the Palazzo Surian on the Cannaregio (Morassi, 1973, cat. 575). Pallucchini pointed out that the figure under the entrance had been drawn on a paper reinforcement, stuck on the original. The letter on the verso, which is

about some agricultural business of the Litta family at Caprarola, does not bear any indication for the dating of the drawing. Goering mentions another letter from Caprarola, dated 20 December 1761, which can be related to a drawing by Guardi in the Metropolitan (1944, 42, fig. 72).

This sheet is a favourite among Guardi's late drawings, for the beauty of its light pen-work and luminous washes.

Francesco Guardi
96. *View of the Grand Canal at S. Geremia*
Inv. no. 196.
Black pencil, pen and brown ink; yellowish
paper on cardboard; 260 x 544 mm.
Inscr.: 'Franco Guardi' (pen, in a nineteenth-
century hand).
Prov.: Correr, 1830.
Lit.: Damerini, 1912, pl. XXXIX; Fiocco,
1929, 572 (Nicolò); Moschini, 1929-30, 308;
Il Settecento Italiano, 1932, fig. 197; Lorenzetti, 1936, no. 27; Pallucchini, 1943, 60,
no. 164 (Nicolò?); Goering, 1944, 41, no. 70;
Byam Shaw, 1951, 61, no. 18; Idem, 1962,
no. 61; Pignatti, 1967, XXII, note; Morassi,
1975, 146, no. 382; Dorigato, 1977, no. 83;
Pignatti, 1983, no. 621.
Exhibitions: Venice, 1929; Venice, 1936;
Venice, 1962; Venice, 1977.
Fiocco first attributed to Nicolò Guardi a
series of drawings of the Correr Museum
with 'long figures, with small heads', very
reminiscent of Canaletto's manner. His
attribution was accepted by Pallucchini, but
it was then rejected when Byam Shaw
pointed out the clear influence of Canaletto
on Francesco Guardi's early views, around
the 1950s and 1960s. Therefore, it was easier
to explain not only the figure types, later
abandoned by Francesco, but also a certain
trend to open out the view's perspective, with
a wide-angle effect, very close to that obtained
by Canaletto with the camera obscura. Later
a certain number of Francesco's drawings 'in
Canaletto's manner' was put together, such
as the large sheets with the Grand Canal in
Cambridge, in the British Museum, in the
Davis collection, London (Morassi, 1975,
cat. 381, 361, 362, 379), and consequently the
Correr series, formerly ascribed to Nicolò,
was attributed to Francesco Guardi's early
period.

There are nine drawings of this type by the
artist in the Correr collection, and three
other ones on the verso of later drawings.
This sheet with S. Geremia was used as a pro-
totype by Byam Shaw, because the building works of the church (begun in 1753)
suggested a dating before the end of the
1750s. Typical is the wide-angle perspective,
which appears also in the painting in the
Frick collection, New York (Morassi, 1973,
cat. 574), depicting the same view.

Francesco Guardi
97. *The Rialto Bridge with Palazzo Manin*
Inv. no. 1197.
Pen and sepia; grey-blue paper;
227 x 161 mm.
Prov.: Correr, 1830. *Lit.:* Pallucchini, 1943,
47, no. 78a; Muraro, 1949, 128; Ragghianti,
1953, 22; Moschini, 1956, fig. III; La peinture

italienne, 1960, no. 304; Pignatti, 1963, 52,
no. 92; Bonicatti, 1964, 141; Pignatti, 1964,
65-6, no. 92; Idem, 1965, 27, no. 89; Idem,
1967, LXVI; Zampetti, 1967, 358, no. 163;
Morassi, 1975, 143, no. 365; Pignatti, 1983,
no. 661.
Exhibitions: Paris, 1960; Washington, 1963;
Venice, 1964; London, 1965; Venice, 1967.
Since the start of the eighteenth century the
view of the Rialto bridge seen from the Riva
del Carbon, with the foreshortening of
Palazzo Manin by Sansovino on the right,
appears very often in Canaletto's paintings,
after that in Woburn Abbey (Constable–
Links, 1976, no. 225), of which Consul Smith

owned a drawing (*ibid.*, no. 591). Francesco
Guardi first adopted this view in the large
painting of Lord Iveagh; the present drawing
is however much later, close in time to the
picture in the Gulbenkian collection, Lisbon
(Morassi, 1973, cat. 524 and 525), and it is
probably connected with a graphic series to
which also belongs the drawing of the Rialto
bridge seen from above, owned by the Ashmolean Museum, Oxford (Morassi, 1975,
cat. 369).

This atmospheric view, with its rapid and
extremely evocative pen strokes, can be
considered a masterpiece in Guardi's late
style.

Francesco Guardi
98. *The Return of the Bucintoro to the S. Andrea Fort*
Inv. no. 60.
Pen and sepia on blue-grey paper; 220 x 400 mm.
Prov.: Zoppetti, 1952. *Lit.:* Damerini, 1912, 51; Lorenzetti, 1936, no. 37; Pallucchini, 1943, 52, no. 101; Ragghianti, 1953, 19, 24, no. 38 (Giacomo?); Pignatti, 1963, 52-3, no. 95 (Giacomo?); Byam Shaw, 1964, 176-82; Pignatti, 1964, 67, no. 95 (Giacomo?); Pignatti, 1967, LX; Morassi, 1975, 128, no. 289; Dorigato, 1977, 70, no. 80; Pignatti, 1983, no. 660.
Exhibitions: Venice, 1936; Washington, 1963; Venice, 1964; Venice, 1977.
It is very difficult sometimes to include some later drawings, often with boats and views of the lagoon, in Francesco Guardi's catalogue. There is a group of sheets, such as the *Views of the Bacino* in the National Gallery, Ottawa and in the Fogg Museum (Morassi, 1975, cat. 343, 401), the Bucintoro in the National Library, Turin (*ibid.*, cat. 283, 284) and the view of the Redentore, formerly in the Ingram collection (*ibid.*, fig. 638, attr. to Giacomo), which show the same style in the thread-like, flickering lines, creating effects of rarefied clearness. The first hypothesis that those drawings were copies by Giacomo Guardi was later rejected (Byam Shaw, 1964, 179), and the series was attributed to Francesco's latest period, to which belong

such masterpieces as the Bucintoro, formerly in the Seilern collection, where the extremely light pen strokes outlining the palaces and the gondolas against transparent washes are among the artist's best expressions (Morassi, 1975, cat. 280). The Correr Bucintoro belongs to this series and it is related to pictures like the Stramezzi Bucintoro of the 1780s (Morassi, 1973, cat. 287).

Even for the present drawing there have been some doubts about the attribution and the hypothesis of Giacomo's intervention has been put forward, owing to the peculiar swarming effect of the figures and their curious pin-shaped heads (Ragghianti, 1953; Pignatti, 1964). However, all the doubts are removed if one compares the present drawing with another Bucintoro certainly by Giacomo, though bearing his father's signature (repr. in Simonson, 1904, 68): definitely more static, flat in the washes progression, and showing the typical hook-shaped figures.

In the Lille Museum there is a Bucintoro, identical in size and style to the present drawing, which was originally its pendant (Morassi, 1975, cat. 282).

Francesco Guardi
99. *The Polignac Wedding Banquet*
Inv. no. 29.
Black pencil, pen and sepia, and coloured washes; 275 x 149 mm.
Inscr.: 'Sala del nobil H. Gradenigo a Carpenedo coll'apparato dei convitati alle nozze del Pollignac' (in the hand of Nicolò Barozzi, 1867?).
Prov.: Zoppetti, 1852. *Lit.:* Damerini, 1912, 52; Idem, 1922, fig. 48; Fogolari, 1924-5, 22; Il Settecento Italiano, 1932; Lorenzetti, 1936, no. 108; Pallucchini, 1943, 51-2, no. 100; Idem, 1947, 68, no. 107; Moschini, 1956, fig. 171; Pallucchini, 1960, 250-1; La peinture italienne, 1960, no. 314; Parker–Byam Shaw, 1962, 72, no. 100; Pignatti, 1963, 51, no. 90; Idem, 1964, 63, no. 88; Idem, 1965, 27-8, no. 93; Idem, 1967, LVII; Zampetti, 1969, 272, no. 123; Pignatti, 1971, pl. p. 71; Morassi, 1975, 134, no. 318; Venezia nell'età di Canova, 1978, no. 44; Dessins Vénitiens, 1983, 178, no. 115; Pignatti, 1983, no. 659.
Exhibitions: Venice, 1929; Venice, 1936; Lausanne, 1947; Paris, 1960; Venice, 1962; Washington, 1963; Venice, 1964; London, 1965; Venice, 1969; Venice, 1978; Bruxelles, 1983.

The Correr owns three drawings showing the Polignac wedding, which took place on September 6, 1790. Francesco Guardi was evidently asked to prepare some paintings to record the event. This is a *modelletto* of the banquet scene, showing the Neoclassical decoration of the hall in the villa Gradenigo. Guardi's late style is characterized by the figures, that are enlarged and closed at the bottom by precise outlines, the small heads rendered with a rapid pen stroke or a touch of brush, the ladies' fanciful hair-styles, and an overall half-surrealistic half-grotesque touch, such as the one which characterizes, for example, the *Concerto di dame* in the Alte Pinakothek, Munich (Morassi, 1973, cat. 256)

Francesco Guardi
100. *The Fenice Theatre*
Inv. no. 724.
Pen and brown ink and sepia wash;
195 x 254 mm.
Inscr.: 'Fenice' (pen, in the artist's hand).
Prov.: Correr, 1830. *Lit.:* Simonson, 1904, 59;
Idem, 1907, 268; Damerini, 1912, 54;
Lapauze and Guarnati, 1919, 187; Fiocco,
1923, fig. 144; Il Settecento Italiano, 1932,
fig. 198; Lorenzetti, 1936, no. 9; Pallucchini,
1943, 49, no. 87; Idem, 1947, 69, no. 188;
Ragghianti, 1953, 22, 24, no. 32; Moschini,
1956, fig. 190; Europäisches Rokoko, 1958,
no. 288; Pallucchini, 1960, 252; La peinture
italienne, 1960, no. 316; Parker–Byam
Shaw, 1962, 57-8, no. 70; Pignatti, 1963, 52,
no. 93; Idem, 1964, 66, no. 93; Fiocco, 1965,
fig. 60; Pignatti, 1965, 28, no. 94; Idem, 1967,
LXVII; Zampetti, 1967, 360, no. 164; Byam
Shaw, 1975, 858; Morassi, 1975, 150,
no. 404; Venezia nell'età di Canova, 1978,
no. 45; Pignatti, 1983, no. 662.
Exhibitions: Venice, 1929; Lausanne, 1947;
Munich, 1958; Paris, 1960; Venice, 1962;

Washington, 1963; Venice, 1964; London,
1965; Venice, 1967; Venice, 1978.
Francesco twice sketched the Fenice theatre,
which was opened on May 16, 1792, a few
months before his death (May 1, 1793); the
second drawing, similar in size, is in the
Metropolitan Museum, New York (Morassi,
1975, cat. 405). This remarkable drawing,
among the artist's last works, synthesizes all
his highest expressive qualities: an extraordinary independence from the architectural
motif, drawn from life but recreated by a
vivid imagination; an airy and almost
impalpable touch, which gives life to the
image of a much-loved landscape.

Giacomo Guardi
101. *View of the Grand Canal at the Rialot*
Inv. no.: 5077.
Black pen and tempera, 108 x 177 mm.
Prov.: Busetto. *Lit.:* Pignatti, 1963, no. 86;
idem, 1964, no. 96; idem, 1965, no. 97;
Dorigato 1977, no. 2.
Many tempera sketches by Giacomo Guardi
are to be found in the Correr, identifiable by
the style of the notes on their back stating the
drawings to be available 'al Ospedaletto in
Calle del Perruchier n. 5245'. Of these, many
of which came to the collection direct from
the artist, this view of the Grand Canal is
typical. Its format suggests that the veduta
was intended for sale to a visitor.

Giacomo's graphic style is clearly
intended to imitate that of his father, and
particularly in background architectural
details achieves almost completely the effect
of Francesco's late sktches. Even if there is
no great difference of type in his 'mark',
Giacomo does nonetheless maintain a trace
of linear regularity derived from Canaletto,
and can be identified by certain involuntary
gestures, similar to hooks or quotation
marks. As to colour, Giacomo does not have
the exquisite transparency of atmosphere
found in his father's work, so that Giacomo's
drawings have a heavy and ponderous feel,
most markedly when the brushwork is
initially coarse in hatching and shading.

Because of the close links to Francesco's
style, the group of drawings to which this one
belongs should probably be dated to the
eighteenth century.

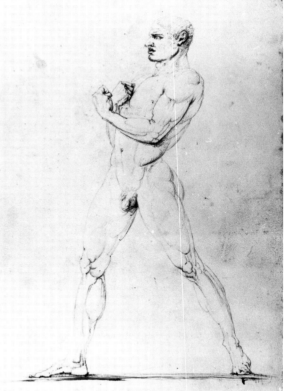

Antonio Canova (1757-1822)
102. *Male Nude Holding his Fist Above his Head* (Creugante)
Inv. no. 5934.
Pen, grey ink on white paper; 454 x 315 mm.
Inscr.: below, on the original *passe-partout* mounting of thick grey-blue paper, the note in Canova's hand: 'In segno di vera stima per la Nobil Sig.ra Francesca Capello, Antonio Canova fece questi quatro segni Roma 1794'.
Prov.: unknown, 1890.

Antonio Canova
103. *Male Nude with his Hand on His Chest* (Damosseno)
Pen, grey ink on white paper; 450 x 315 mm.
Inscr.: below, on the original *passe-partout* mounting of thick grey-blue paper, the note in Canova's hand: 'In segno di vera stima per la Nobil Sig.ra Francesca Capello, Antonio Canova fece questi quatro segni Roma 1794'.
[As above.]
Prov.: unknown, 1890. *Lit.:* Bratti, 1917,

no. 11; Bassi, 1959, pp. 78-79; Pavanello, 1976, nos. 126 and 129, and 1978, nos. 100 and 101; Rigon, 1982, nos. 89 and 191.
This pair of drawings concerns the conception and the first working-out of the two famous statues of Creugante and Damosseno in the Vatican Museums. The drawings, mentioned by Bratti (1917, no. 11, p. 436), are very similar to others in Bassano and Treviso, especially that of Creugante, no. 622 of 7 November, 1794, dating from the same period, as Pavanello points out (1976, no. 126). The statues corresponding to the drawings were executed at different times, *Creugante* in 1796 and *Damosseno* in 1802-1806, and were controversially received by contemporary critics. The two works, which Pavanello describes as being 'among the most carefully thought-out of Canova's sculptures', were inspired by Pausanias's narrative of an episode in the Nemean Games, and certainly derive from similar sculptural or decorative antique groups, particularly from the *Tyrannicides* in Naples and the *Dioscuri* in Monte Cavallo. The drawings in the Correr bear dedications in

Canova's hand to Francesca Cappello, wife of Antonio, who was one of Canova's greatest admirers. Though they are described with ostentatious modesty as 'four sketches', the studies are actually of the greatest interest and the highest quality among Canova's drawings (the drawing of Damosseno shows signs of some significant changes introduced by the artist in the course of his work), and they also serve to underline his interest in 'tragic' subjects and forceful handling, together with the mythological and allegorical themes Canova had already abundantly treated in pursuit of a prevalently sentimental and 'graceful' elegance. At the same time as he was working on the two 'Boxers', Canova was working on the episodes of *Hercules Shooting his Children* (in various interpretations) and of *Hercules and Lyca*, the colossal group now in the Gallery of Modern Art in Rome.

Antonio Canova
104. *Nude Male Weeping*
Inv. no. 5478.
Pen, sepia on white paper; 445 x 309 mm.
Original *passe-partout* mounting on thick
dark paper.
Inscr.: below left, autograph note: 'All'amico
Dottor Aglietti Antonio Canova fece questi
due segni'. [For his friend Doctor Aglietti,
Antonio Canova made these two sketches.]
Prov.: unknown, 1877. *Lit.:* Pavanello, 1976,
no. D.20 and 1978, no. 102.
The drawing is dedicated in Canova's hand
to the Brescian doctor, Francesco Aglietti,
who held positions of the highest cultural
importance in Venice and also attended
Canova on his deathbed. There is an identical
autograph copy of it in a private Venetian
collection (Pavanello, 1976, no. D.20), and it
is also chronologically linked with the painting of Cephalus and Procris in the Possagno
Gypsoteca, which is comparable with
Girodet's celebrated *Atlas*. Cephalus's
desperation on finding that he has unwittingly
killed his beloved Procris is expressed in the
body of the weeping figure with an impas-
sioned anatomical insight, which Canova
handles, as always, with a simplicity of
drawing that is almost elementary, while
displaying an expert and effective draughtsmanship.

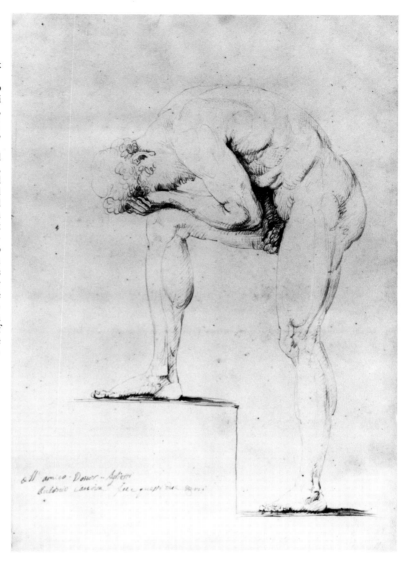

Antonio Canova
105. *Study for the Three Graces*
Inv. no. Album 74, no. 7.
Pencil on white paper; 200 x 111 mm.
Prov.: Gamba, 1841.
106. *Study for the Three Graces*
Inv. no.: no. 74, no. 8.
Pencil on white paper; 172 x 92 mm.
Prov.: Gamba, 1841. *Lit.:* Pavanello, 1976,
no. 270 (4 and 5) and 1978, nos. 141 and
141b; Rigon, 1982, no. 200.

Canova perfectly handled the exquisitely
symbolic, and programmatically Neoclassical
theme of the Three Graces, above all in his
famous marble group in the Leningrad
Hermitage, and in the replica he made – also
in marble – for the Duke of Bedford at
Woburn Abbey. The Leningrad group had
been commissioned from the artist by
Giuseppina Beauharnais and, after her
death, her son Eugéne, ex-Viceroy of Italy,
took it with him into exile in Munich.

The group is one of Canova's most celebrated works, and was among his most
successful both with critics (though there
was some disagreement) and the public. It is
regarded as a work of great innovative force
(the models, as Pavanello observes, do not
follow the traditional arrangements of
antiquity) and of a very powerful and
admirable aesthetic message. The two
drawings in the Correr collection come from
the album of the learned Venetian librarian
Bartolomeo Gamba, who wrote a successful
series of lives of the artists and writers of his
time. The most finished drawing (no. 106)
already shows the definition of the final
arrangement of the marble group to a high
degree, even if the body of the girl to the right
seems less rotated; the drapery is held in the
left hand of the central figure and wrapped
around the girl on the right, whereas in the
finished group it falls well within the central
space enclosed by the three bodies. The
faces, however, look towards the observer
instead of interweaving their glances as they
do in the finished work.

This last remark is perhaps the most
important clue towards establishing the
drawing within the artist's itinerary from his
first idea for the group to the final result. The
girls are still infused with gracefulness and
elegant sensuality, and are still *à la mode* (as
we can see in their hairstyles, sketched with
little tangled lines); they stare incuriously
and brazenly from the little sketch, freeing
themselves progressively from all mundane
connotations, to interweave a taut dialogue
of tones that are calibrated to the point of
being pathetic and sorrowful; in this way,
they embody the sublime ideals of beauty
that would almost make them into an artistic
manifesto of the highest evocative power.

Antonio Canova
107. *Study for the Tomb of the Contessa di Santa Cruz*
Inv. no. Album 77, no. 33.
Pencil on white paper; 190 x 251 mm.
Inscr.: on the album mounting (f. 33) in L. Cicognara's hand: 'Primo studio del monumento della M.sa di Santa Cruz. Canova'.
Prov.: Cicognara, 1885. *Lit.:* A. Gonzales Palacios, 1972, pp. 160-167; Pavanello, 1976, nos. 195 and 196, no. 343a.

This drawing is connected to Canova's preliminary work for the tomb and sarcophagus of the Countess of Santa Cruz and her daughter, (the wife of the Marquis de Haro, Great Chamberlain to Joseph Bonaparte, King of Spain) who died respectively in 1803 and 1806. Because of his client's fall into disgrace, the tomb was never completed. The drawing – from the Cicognara Album – shows some differences from the gesso and the marble models, which are both in Possagno.

The marble was admired by Canova's contemporaries as one of the most successful representations of the pathetic and the sublime in any funerary monument, and so moved and delighted Cicognara that Canova made him a present of the sketch.

In this sketch the configuration of the setting is still in the process of being established, although all the main elements included in the final work are present.

Canova exchanged the standing and kneeling female figures for those of the dead Countess's husband and brothers, which eliminated any element of allegory from the mourning group, and turned the scene into a more credible and moving family circle.

The drawing is executed in a hasty and schematic manner, though it presents some typical and recurrent themes of Canova's mature style, such as the kneeling figures.

Antonio Canova
108. *Dancers*
Inv. no. Album 77, no. 35.
Pencil on white paper; 205 x 248 mm.
Pasted onto a page of heavy grey paper with a border and the inscription: 'Primi studi delle sue danzatrici, e scherzi, poi pubblicati colle stampe. Canova'. [First studies of his dancers, and sketches, later published among his engravings.]
Prov.: Cicognara, 1885. *Lit.:* Gonzales Palacios, 1972; Pavanello, 1978, no. 343b.
These 'preliminary studies' of dancers are also taken from the Cicognara Album. These dancers belong to the group of Canova's drawings which, according to Gonzales Palacios, 'reflect the more feminine, less engagé aspect of his complex personality', and should be taken in series with the many analogous studies among the papers in the Bassano Museum (cf. Rigon, 1982, *passim*) and, with the others, 'were to lead to the charming *Dancers*, counted among the

sculptor's most valued marbles' and which best bear evidence of his 'antiquarian' period (Gonzales Palacios).
Chronologically, this drawing belongs to the period of Canova's work (at Possagno) in tempera on a black ground (Pavanello); and compared with other analogous drawings, it is still very schematic but not lacking in grace, especially in the figure of the dancer.

Andrea Appiani (1754-1817)
109. *Portrait of Eugène de Beauharais*
Inv. no. Album 77, 5 bis.
Pastel on Havana-brown paper; 155 x 119 mm.
Inscr.: at the right 'Appiani'; below 'Eugenio Beauharnais' in the hand of L. Cicognara.
Prov.: Cicognara, 1885. *Lit.:* Nicodemi, 1944; Gonzales Palacios, 1967; Precerutti Gerberi, 1969-70; Idem, 1970, pp. 138-142; Idem, 1970, pp. 13-26; Pavanello, 1978, no. 339.
The portrait of the Viceroy of Italy and Prince of Venice, the son of Giuseppina Beauharnais, is 'one of Andrea Appiani's most beautiful drawings', according to Gonzales Palacios, and belongs to the album of Leopoldo Cicognara.
It is a pastel-drawing of the highest quality and a vibrant and sensitive immediacy, and shows all of Appiani's mastery as a painter and portraitist even in this small format and its almost domestic and intimate connotations.

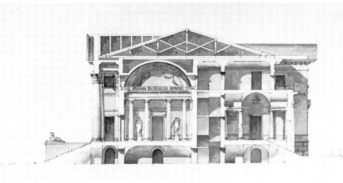

Giacomo Quarenghi (1744-1817)
110/111. *Country House of Prince Kovrikin,
Cross-section and Front Elevation*
Inv. no. 6166.

a. Pen and brush; Indian ink and watercolour on white paper; 446 x 594 mm.
Inscr.: below, in pencil, 'Façade de la Maison
de Campagne di M. Le Prince Kovrokin etc.
du Coté du Jardin, pour M. Selva'.
Prov.: Wcowich-Lazzari, 1896.

Inv. no. 6165.

b. Pen, brush; Indian ink and watercolour on
white card.
Prov.: Wcowich-Lazzari, 1896. *Lit.:* Mioni,
1935; Lo Gatto, 1943, 111.

These drawings came to the Correr among
the material from Selva's hand in the
Wcowich-Lazzari collection.

We can therefore assume, as Gamba says,
that they were the plans that the Venetian
architect – who had a longstanding and
reciprocal friendship with Quarenghi – had
hanging in his studio as exemplary models
for his students.

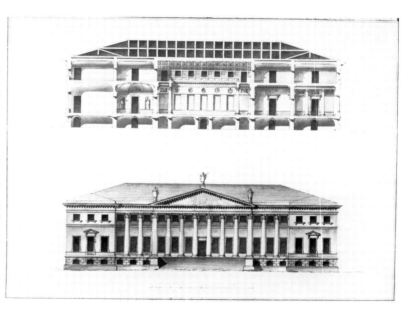

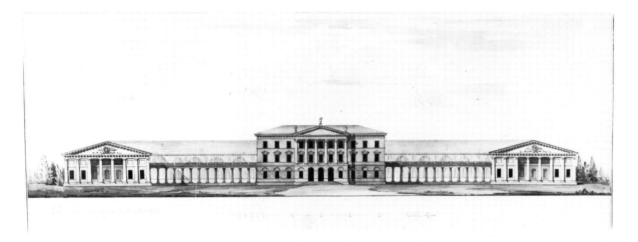

The two drawings show the frontal elevations and the longitudinal and transverse cross-sections of the house – which is clearly of a Palladian inspiration – designed for the dignitary named in the pencil inscription. This building is apparently less monumental and gigantic than some of Quarenghi's other city or country palaces (the Palace of Prince Bezborodkho in Moscow, for instance) and it shows, if anything, some similarity in conception with the 'English' palace of Peterhof. Above all, though, the building shows the architect's intention of preserving the compactness of formulation and structural unity of a town house, more than of a country house set in a park.

The quality of the two drawings is very fine, good enough, in fact, to dispel any doubt about whether they were from Quarenghi's hand – see the sketches of the statues in the acroteria.

The villa is recognisably quadrilateral in structure, with a large central gallery in two orders, spanned by a barrel-vault, and with *loggette* on its shorter sides. The tympanum of the principle façade does not protrude, and neither do the two lateral parts that close off the rear façade, presenting an identical configuration on both faces of the villa.

The large collections of Quarenghi's drawings in Bergamo, Venice and Russia lack any other references to this project, which must therefore have been an isolated and unique event.

Giacomo Quarenghi (1744-1817)
112. *Bank in St. Petersburg*
Inv. no. 6168.
Pen, brush, Indian ink and watercolour on white paper; 207 x 514 mm.
Inscr.: below, left, 'Façade de la Banque de Saint Petersbourg'. Scale in Russian measurements; 'Pour M;r Alessandri da consegnare'.
Prov.: Wcowich-Lazzari, 1896. *Lit.:* Mioni, 1935; Lo Gatto, 1943; Catalogo Mostra Quarenghi, 1967, no. 93.
This drawing concerns the celebrated project for the State Bank, created by Catherine II and commissioned from Quarenghi in 1781. According to his son Giulio Quarenghi in 1821, it was 'the first great work that Catherine commissioned from Quarenghi'. With its scholarly method of composition, which can also be seen in the large blueprint, the building apparently expresses the architect's extraordinary capacity to create highly original *invenzioni*, even making use of the Neoclassical lexicon, in his first and very convincing attempts at an independent manner, even though it falls within the great tradition of classical architecture.

The drawing is dedicated to the otherwise unidentified Alessandri, and is perfectly comparable with the lower part of drawing H-56 in the great collection of Quarenghi's drawings in the Civic Library in Bergamo (*Disegni*, 1967, no. 93). It seems likely to be from Quarenghi's hand, given the fine quality of its line and watercolour and the fresh immediacy of the effect of the whole. On the other hand, even if we were to agree with Mioni in considering it, along with the whole group of Quarenghi's drawings in the Correr, to be a copy by Selva, and just because it can be traced back to a highly significant building within Quarenghi's planning activity in Russia and assigned to a Venetian environment, it is very likely that Quarenghi had wanted personally to supervise or at least to follow its execution.

Giannantonio Selva (1751-1818)
Mont Cenis Monument
113. *Vertical Cross-section*
Inv. no. 6288.
Pen and brush, Indian ink and watercolour;
504 x 745 mm.
Prov.: Wcowich-Lazzari, 1896.

114. *Elevation*
Inv. no. 6287.
Pen and brush, Indian ink and watercolour.
Scale in French feet.
Prov.: Wcowich-Lazzari, 1896. *Lit.:* Missirini,
1823; Etlin, 1894; Blanchard, 1917; Bratti,
1917-18; Bassi, 1936; Alberici, 1963; Hubert,
1964; Mezzanotte, 1966; Brusatin, 1969;
Oechslin, 1971; *The Age of Neoclassicism*,
1972; *Giuseppe Pistocchi*, 1974; Godoli, 1974;
Patetta, 1975; Dezzi Bardeschi, 1976;
Romanelli, 1977 and 1978.

Giannantonio Selva worked out the project
for a monument to commemorate the French
Army's crossing of the Alps before Marengo,
and the construction of a road between
Savoy and Susa across Mont Cenis (the
whole matter is described by Hubert, 1961

and Dezzi Bardeschi, 1976), faithfully
following the directions given by the
Commission which had been set up by the
Academy of Milan, and producing two

different and very dissimilar versions. One,
inspired by the Temple of Vesta, developed
the theme of a mausoleum built on a symmet-
rical plan in the form of a cylindrical tower

surrounded by an open gallery – a 'temple of Glory', as Canova called it in a letter to his friend dated 21 August 1813 – and standing in a square water-filled area marked off by boundaries and minor buildings. The other, shown in these drawings, aimed at an 'absolutist' intention, which was decidedly close to the researches begun above all in Rome in the French Academy and gathered from all the major European architects and theorists from the middle of the eighteenth century, especially in relation to commemorative and sepulchral themes, and to the suggested possibility of combing the Neo-Egyptian with the Neo-Grecian styles. With all these connotations, Selva's pyramidal monument is closer to those of the 'visionary' architects than to any others.

Selva's dislike for monumentalism made him reluctant to join the Milanese commission set up to plan a work that he considered to be alien to his tastes and intentions. The project for the Cenesio monument in the form of a temple to Glory – which was abandoned on Canova's explicit advice in favour of a pyramid – was a weak and decidedly academic work, whereas the pyramid project shows more vigour and conviction, although we must remark once again that the abstract theme was much less suitable to Giannantonio's tastes than the cunning contextual integration of buildings or the solution of difficult problems of organization and arrangement.

Both of the typologies that Selva approved had a long tradition, especially in academic projects, as it has been pointed out and as it may be verified by comparison with the designs of the French Academy in Rome, for example. But one should note that the same directive to which Selva conformed, encouraged him towards derivative or even obvious solutions: even Canova, who received copies of the two projects, commended his friend but noted that he himself 'had come at once to the same conclusion, together with some of our other Roman academics'.

Selva's drawings are of high quality, though perhaps better in the finely water-coloured elevation than in the more academic view of the cross-section. As an illustrator of his own architectural ideas, Selva shows the influence of the French school in accordance with a taste and a technique of drawing imported and spread by the precepts of the reformed Accademie di Belli Arti. By the very fact of his holding the Chair of Architecture at the Venetian Academy, Selva was to influence further generations of Venetian architects.

Leopoldo Pollack (1751-1806)
115. *Elevation of a Small Temple*
Inv. no. 8238.
Pen, black ink and watercolour; 355 x 475 mm.
Inscr.: Autograph inscription with signature 'Leopoldo Pollack Reg.o Arch. to 1799'. Marca c.s.
Prov.: Musatti, 1967; Ottino Della Chiesa, 1959, no. 57. *Lit.:* Mezzanotte, 1966, no. 115; Pignatti, 1970-71, no. 44.
The drawing, published by Ottino Della Chiesa in 1957, no. 57, and in Pignatti's catalogue of 1970-71, no. 44, is signed and dated 1799. Pollack signs himself 'royal architect' and so it is likely that this drawing is connected to the Austrian period before the second Cisalpine Republic and Napoleon's decisive advent in Milan – and Pollack's consequent fall into political disfavour. This drawing comes close in its graphic handling and stylistic characterisation to other projects that Pollack designed for the Belgioioso estate at Zagonara, near Pavia, for example the Sundial, signed and dated 1800 and also in the Musatti Collection held in the Correr. In particular, we should note its connection with the sketch (dated 1796) in the Bertarelli collections in Milan (Mezzanotte, 1966, no. 115), which shows a *cella* distinguished on the outside by 'two unidentified sections made up of all kinds of fragments, arranged in disorder and confusion'. This drawing shows an identical theme and its consequent working-out, in spite of the evident differences, especially in the solution to the access-doorway. This taste for romantic ruins, and the allusion to the passage of time, allegorized precisely through the 'fragments' in 'disorder and confusion', is well-suited to

Pollack's predisposition towards the English style of garden, no less than to the impending and particularly Milanese 'cemeterial' themes of the Neoclassical era.

rapidity of handling, showing that drawing is a primary component in his art, but demonstrating above all that he is never overwhelmed by the more formalized and recurrent elements in the decorative and conventional language of Neoclassicism.

Giuseppe Bernardino Bison
117. *Hurdy-gurdy Players and Countrywomen*
Inv. no. 1814.
Black pencil retraced with pen and dark brown ink, sepia wash; grey-blue paper; 142 x 192 mm.
Inscr.: below right: 'Bisson' (autograph).
Prov.: Gamba, 1841. *Lit.:* Morandotti, 1942, no. 37; Rizzi, 1962, nos. 62 and 89; Pignatti, 1980, no. 39.
Pignatti describes this lively drawing by Bison as 'an evocative and somewhat mysterious gypsy subject'. Traced in pen over a previous pencil foundation, it exhibits a very varied network of line in which a rapid treatment of shading follows a style of recurrent and winding curves.

There is no lack of famous precedents both for the idea and for the preparation of the scene: some broadly Tiepolesque influences, according to Pignatti, are possibly mingled with sixteenth-century suggestions in the manner of Campagnola. The lowered point of view and the foreground position of the figures that reduces the background to the minimum for the context and the setting, is naturally effective, and the coincidence of the roofline and of the more distant and barely-sketched-in landscape with the posture of the agile figure of the musician, is also successful.

The drawing may be compared, for its subject and its stylistic notation, with the one in the Castello Sforzesco A/341/693 (cf. Rizzi, 1962, no. 89) and with that in the drawing of *Two Women Spinning* in the Trieste collection (Rizzi, 1962, no. 62). The musician may be considered preparatory to, or at least be put in relation with, the one in the *Tavern-interior* in a private collection in Trento (Morandotti, 1942, no. 37, fig. 35).

Giuseppe Bernardino Bison (1762-1844)
116. *Three Countrywomen*
Inv. no. 754.
Black pencil, pen and brush, dark brown ink; brownish paper mounted on card; 240 x 173 mm.
Prov.: Correr, 1830. *Lit.:* Rizzi, 1962-63, no. 61; Pignatti, 1980, no. 37.
This drawing seems to be one of the not infrequent bucolic monuments in G. Bison's graphic work, and shows the artist's extraordinary versatility and his consummate technique in the use of mottling. This versatility allows him to draw characteristics and cadences of differing and very remote origins and stylistic moulds with great virtuosity,

and to bring them within his own horizons and manner of drawing. He invokes the seventeenth-century Venetian tradition of Tiepolo and Pellegrini, and a certain taste for ruins and caprices that originates in Ricci; but there are also suggestions from the landscape painters and even echoes from the visionary style of Piranesi. We find all this – and the results are surprising – with the spread and establishment of the taste and stylization of Neoclassicism, thinking for example of the drawings of Felice Giani or Andrea Appiani.

Even in such a full and unprejudiced experience of figurative periods and cadences, Bison always retains his great freedom and

Giuseppe Bernardino Bison
118. *Landscape with Fortress and Ferry-Boat*
Inv. no. N. Album 77, no. 11.
Coloured tempera on prepared paper, mounted on card; 137 x 241 mm.
Prov.: Cicognara, 1885. *Lit.:* Gonzales Palacios, 1970; Pignatti, 1980, no. 41.
One of the reasons for the great evocativeness of this tempera originates in its ambiguous combination of reminiscences of Ricci and Zais, and suggestions that are appreciably touched by Romanticism.

There are many references in the drawing to a number of Bison's other landscapes in tempera and gouache, shown in several exhibitions held in stages and devoted to the painter's work (cf. Morandotti, 1942) which confirm, among other things, Bison's receptiveness to eighteenth-century Venetian and Veneto painting, which are midway between an interest in the weather, the allegorical and naturalistic representation of the seasons, and genre scenes.

Giovanni Carlo Bevilacqua (1775-1849)
119. *Three Dancers with Flowers, Leaves and Ribbon*
Inv. no. 4117.
Pen, dark-brown ink and watercolour; 231 x 344 mm.
Inscr.: below left, 'Bevilacqua F. 1801'.
Prov.: Cicogna, 1865. *Lit.:* Pavanello, 1973, p. 25, no. 108, fig. 25; Idem, 1978, no. 181.
This drawing, as Pavanello correctly noted (1973 and 1978, no. 181) is imitated from the famous *Antiquities at Herculaneum*, and seems, like other analogous or identical ones, to be a preparatory sketch for fresco decorations, placed as usual in the centre of an empty background surrounded by grotesques. Signed and dated 1800, this and similar studies seem to stand at the beginning of Bevilacqua's second and more mature period of artistic production, accomplished under the influence of Canova, and by this time coming into line with an 'international' taste, in which 'a rapid, uninterrupted line describes the outlines of images that compose themselves in formal rhythms of a Neo-Alexandrian elegance' (Pavanello, 1973). Pavanello also acutely points out that 'the human figure is reduced to a decorative cypher, almost a "sign" for ornamentation in the industrial arts'. Bevilacqua's innovations are by now effectively placed outside the late-eighteenth-century and Venetian

horizons; on the linguistic side, Bevilacqua fully achieves the poetics of line and abandons the problem of colour (if more, perhaps, in his practice of decoration than in his treatises on aesthetics), and seems to attempt to attain the complete mastery of a lexicon of drawing in which the qualifying choices of Neo-classical iconography are interlaced with a stylistic refinement that reaches the limits of an allusive formalization and becomes, in essence, almost abstract.

Giovanni Carlo Bevilacqua
120. *Allegorical scene*
Inv. no. 4130.
Pen, dark brown ink and watercolour;
270 x 398 mm.
Prov.: Cicogna, 1865. *Lit.:* Pavanello, 1973,
p. 15, no. 31; Idem, 1978, no. 183.
This complex allegorical scene, depicting
Time (below right), winged Genii, Apollo (?)
and other figures set against a grandiose
background of classical architecture, creates
a narrative episode within a vaguely indicated
scenographic structure reminiscent of Pietro
Gonzaga (Pavanello). In comparison with
the more abstract and simplified decorative
scenes or with particular sketches and
portraits in a style and taste of drawing that is
more in the English manner (both considered
to be more in keeping with Bevilacqua's
capacity), this drawing seems to be over-
involved and emphatic in certain aspects.
The self-confident gracefulness of the small
central figures actually shows some contrast
with the more awkward and hidebound
conventionality of the group to the left and of
the winged figure of Time itself.

This drawing, like the previous one, was
donated to the Correr in 1865 by
Emmanuele Cicogna, who came into
possession of the painter's legacy.

Giuseppe Borsato (1770-1849)
121. *Design for fireplace and furnishings for the
Palazzo Reale in Venice*
Inv. no. 6136.
Pen and brush, black ink and watercolour on
white paper, very below to the right;
826 x 556 mm.
Prov.: Wcowich-Lazzari, 1896. *Lit.:* Percier-
Fontaine, 1843, no. 8; Gonzales Palacios,
1976, pp. 44 and 48; Pavanello, 1976, p. 14
and 1978, no. 258.
This is an ornamental design with a great
and refined monumental spirit, which
Borsato produced with an eye to the French
designers (and in particular to Percier and
Fontaine whose work he had studied and
faithfully followed). Although Gonzales
Palacios dated the drawing to 1807, Pavanello
proposes to postpone the dating to 1813-15;
however, Zanotto's evidence – drawn from
the notes commenting on Borsato's *Planches*
that are added to the Italian edition, edited
by Lazzari in Venice in 1843 of the *Recueil* of
Percier and Fontaine – refers explicitly to
1807. Furthermore, Borsato worked actively
almost to the end of his life on the decorations in the so-called *Ala Napoleonica* which,
with the Procuratie Nuove were both transformed, with the building of the Library of
San Marco, into the Imperial palace in

Venice and into apartments for the court.

The elements of the furnishings and the
surroundings to the fireplace itself are of
great interest (that is unusually placed under
a window in an unspecified room in the
palace, as one can confirm from the view of
S. Giorgio through the window): vases,
candlesticks, a clock with the figures of
Mercury, Time and the Hours, 'one of the
artist's most brilliant inventions for the
furnishings of the Royal Palace', according
to Pavanello, and 'exquisitely coloured', but
as far as decoration is concerned, 'in the
outdated manner of Louis XVI, and very
Frenchified', according to Gonzales Palacios
(p. 48), but it seems to us that the high quality
of drawing and the fineness of the detail
correspond to the official nature of the
project (which remained unfulfilled, according to Zanotti, *Recueil*, p. 117), while the
actual quotations (suppressed in the engraved
and published edition) tend to underline a
sort of anthological collection of erotic and
literary figurative themes, which were
appropriate for an intimate and enclosed
area for conversation.

Giuseppe Borsato
122. *Swearing the Oath of Loyalty to Francis I of Austria*
Inv. no. 6443.
Pen and brush, black ink and watercolour on yellowish paper mounted on card; 561 x 881 mm.
Prov.: Roberti, 1936. *Lit.:* Cicognara, 1818; Cicogna, 1847, no. 4648; Malamani, 1888; Bratti, 1917; Brunetti, 1952, p. 11; Ivanoff, 1971, p. 117; Perocco–Salvadori, 1976, fig. 1448; Pavanello, 1978, no. 335; Romanelli, 1983, p. 147.

Borsato's large drawing is only partially in watercolour, and shows the ceremony of swearing the oath to the emperor – and through him to the Archduke Giovanni Battista – by the Venetian nobility in San Marco on 7 May, 1815, after the final defeat of Napoleon and on the occasion of the official establishment of Austrian power in Venice.

The general return to order achieved by this ceremony (and in Borsato's related illustration) was important in a number of ways: one was the definitive official recognition of the basilica of San Marco in its public function, as Napoleonic ecclesiastical policy in Venice had wished, when they had decided to transfer the seat of patriarchal authority from San Pietro di Castello to San Marco.

The composition of the scene still seems strongly influenced by the official court painting of the Napoleonic era, especially in the foreground scenes and in the arrangement of the onlooking women who are drawn up strictly in ranks on the improvised stages set up under the lateral naves. The arrangement of the troops in the central area of the drawing is even colder and more static.

This work was possibly a study or an elaborated preparatory drawing – as Pavanello rightly suggests – for the painting that Borsato was to include in the group of works that Leopoldo Cicognara took to Vienna on the occasion of the fourth marriage of Francis I of Austria in 1817, as an act of homage from the Venetian provinces to Carolina Augusta of Bavaria, the new Imperial consort (there is an engraving by Martens in the volume edited by Cicognara).

The study is rather rigid and schematic in the architectural parts, but is pleasantly animated in the small foreground figures and demonstrates Borsato's mastery both of compositions that are staged on a vast scale, closer to scenographic and theatrical design (ornamentation and scene-painting both in the Venetian and Roman styles were important to Borsato's personality as an artist) than to eighteenth-century Venetian view-painting. In his studies and sketches, Borsato used to make several versions of finished works, according to the wishes of his private or official patrons.

139

Francesco Hayez (1791-1882)
123. *Leopoldo Cicognara*
Inv. no. A 77, no. 73.
Pencil on white paper; 212 x 164 mm.
Inscr.: below, in pencil 'Leopoldo Cicognara'.
Prov.: Cicognara, 1885. *Lit.:* Pavanello, 1978, nos. 347 and 348; Mazzocca, 1983, no. 2.
This little drawing forms part of one of the most interesting and unusual private collections of Neoclassical drawings, the Album of drawings and works by various contemporary artists that Leopoldo Cicognara collected and gave to his second wife Lucia Fantinati, and which is now in the collection of drawings in the Correr Museum. Pavanello and Mazzocca regard it as a preparatory study for the painting in a private Venetian collection that shows the Cicognara family standing beside a colossal portrait of Canova.

On the basis of this identification, as well as for obvious stylistic reasons, the drawing can be dated to around 1816, in the years during which Hayez was living and working in Rome under the direct protection and control of Canova: Canova and Cicognara had been among the first to discover and appreciate Hayez's work as a young man.

In spite of a certain conventional and academic manner (both in the style and posture of the subject and in the cross-hatched shading in the drawing) the portrait seems very effective in revealing the sensitive psychology of the great scholar and patron of the arts Leopoldo Cicognara, who was certainly one of the most prominent figures in the world of the arts and cultural institutions both in the Napoleonic and the Habsburg eras in Europe.

Eugenio Bosa (1807-1875)
124. *The Fisherwoman, sketch*
Inv. no. vol. XIV, no. 139.
Pencil, black ink and brush with sepia ink on white paper (detail of the central figure in a cap); 295 x 405 mm.
Inscr.: above in pencil '15 maggio 1836' (in Bosa's hand).
Prov.: Bosa, 1876.

125. *The Fisherwoman*
Inv. no. Album 42, no. 343.
Pencil, pen, watercolour on white paper; 260 x 353 mm.
Prov.: Bosa, 1876. *Lit.:* Locatelli, v. IV, 1837 (XIII); Nani Mocenigo, 1916[3], pp. 231-32; Damerini, 1971.

The two drawings come from two different albums of Bosa's, and refer to the treatment of a single subject; the drawings differ in the degree of finish as well as in the quality of the work; while no. 125, which is signed, is more complete and refined, and shows the painter's most elaborate work, the other, taken from an album of sketches and working drawings, resembles the sub-Canovan manner that Bosa adopted from time to time in making finished copies for his many clients. If the album of finished drawings could be said to constitute a sort of 'showpiece' to be shown to potential customers, the other – and the many tiny sketches and *macchiette* collected in it – is really a private archive that the artist turned to for the construction of his most successful scenes.

The two drawings should also be considered as preparations for the painting of *The Fisherwoman* that Jacopo Treves de Bonfili commissioned from the painter and which was presented at the public exhibition at the Academy of Fine Arts in 1836, and was favourably reviewed by Locatelli on 19 August: 'in spite of the tiny proportions, the painter records the most beautiful outlines and a perfect composition, enlivened by his splendid palette' (also in *L'Appendice*, IV, 1837, XIII, pp. 195-96).

The subject is one that was dear and congenial to Bosa: he was inspired by daily life, by indigence and poverty, and by the habits, customs and occupations of the people of Venice and Chioggia. Indeed, the poorest and humblest reality, and the outright ragged and beggarly poverty of the minor centres of the lagoon, certainly helped Bosa and other Venetian painters to introduce a sketchy and superficial element of 'genre' and realism into their work, in opposition to the morass of mythological and academic subjects or the historical painting that was more in fashion at the time.

The sketch displays Eugenio Bosa's great skill and his illustrative gifts (see a variant in

sepia in the same album XIV, no. 17, with details in pencil), while he becomes pedantic, didactic and lachrymose in his finished watercolours, and even more so in his oil-paintings.

Bosa is regarded as a didactic and moralizing painter, and can be regarded as a transitional element towards the concentration on the poor in the realistic painting of the following decades.

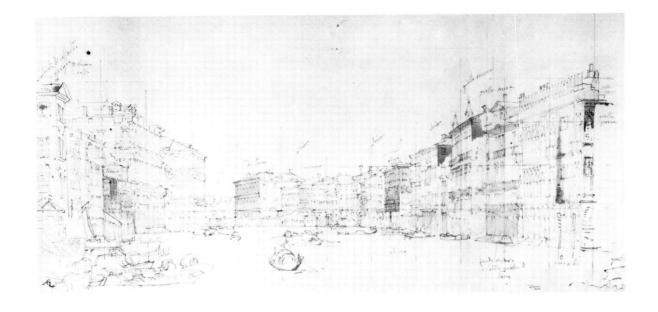

Ippolito Caffi (1809-1866)
126. *View of Venice*
Inv. no. 5982.
Pencil and watercolour on white paper; 246 x 374 mm. Traces of grid-lines in pencil.
Prov.: Caffi.

The traces of a pencil grid show that this sketch was to be used more fully for one or more paintings. The panorama of the Riva degli Schiavoni – in which his masterpiece was his view from the Ponte della Veneta Marina in 1858 (Perocco, 1979, no. 112) – is shown here in a watercolour of great immediacy that is summary in its drawing, and handled with agility in the area of the *squerci*, (the naval buildings backing onto the Rio dell'Arsenale). A sort of pendant in reverse is to be found in the painting which shows the Riva drawn from the Library of San Marco as far as the Giardini di Castello (1865; Perocco, 1979, no. 120), but Caffi also gives drawings of the Bacino di San Marco from other points of view as well as in his much-admired versions in lithograph.

In this unpublished drawing, Caffi has found a means of fixing his attention on the great masted vessels that always serve to animate an otherwise conventional fixity in his Venetian panoramas, when they are not transfigured by his use of particular atmospheric 'filters' or unusual meteorological effects.

Ippolito Caffi
127. *The Grand Canal at the Ca' d'Oro*
Inv. no. 5982.
Black pencil and watercolour on white paper; 260 x 452 mm.
Inscr.: various notes on colour, squared up in red ink.
Prov.: Caffi. *Lit.:* Perocco, 1979.

This fine drawing, like the previous one, is a preparatory drawing for a painting, as can be seen both from the notes on coloration and from the squaring-up of the sheet, and recalls certain eighteenth-century effects of drawing in the style of Bellotto (whom Caffi certainly regarded as a point of reference, and followed devotedly).

The point of view is largely at the same height as the Palazzo Da Mosto, and extends as far as there, as well as reaching the area enclosed on the left by the two buildings of the Ca' Corner della Regina and the Ca'Pesaro, and on the right by the palazzata that extends from the Ca' d'Oro to the Palazzo Loredan Vendramin Calergi – the area of San Marcuola.

The liveliness of the boats and the merchandise in the Rialto market in the foreground, serves to counterpoint the scenes of daily working-life against the monumentality in certain areas butting onto the Grand Canal. It is remarkable that to find analogies to this sort of drawing by Caffi one must seek outside the Venetian circle as far as the contemporary drawings of Vervloet or to the nimble and highly accurate Venetian notes

of Ruskin and his draughstmen and followers, also in Venice.

Ippolito Caffi
128. *Arabic Customs*
Inv. no. 5981/24.
Pencil and watercolour on light-brown paper; 290 x 453 mm.
Inscr.: above right: 'Le tende degli Arabi sono alte sette piedi non piu' [The tents of the Arabs are not more than seven feet high]; below right: 'Memorie di costumi Arabi. Caffi dis.o'.
Prov.: Caffi.

This large unpublished drawing is datable to the months of 1843 and 1844 in which Caffi went to Malta, Athens, Constantinople, Smyrna, Ephesus, Alexandria and Cairo. From here he was able to travel up the Nile as far as Luxor and Karnak, and to reach Nubia, from where he turned towards Jerusalem and Asia Minor.

Many sketches survive from these travels – as well as oil-paintings – in notebooks and loose leaves, both of landscapes and costumes, figures and animals that on the one hand are fully attributable to the travel-records of Orientalist painters who were active and prolific throughout the nineteenth century, and on the other hand they reveal the keen and unusual attention that the painter paid to his own rapid sketches, impressions and sensations that were often motivated more by personal curiosity and by the desire to sketch from memory than by the wish to prepare studies for canvases, to be developed at a later date.

This drawing seems sufficiently detailed and precise to allow us to speculate that Caffi wished to produce a later version in oils.

The figure on the left carrying an amphora inevitably recalls similar subjects in Neo-classical and academic works, but a desire prevails, in spite of any other possible intentions, to animate a scene that is both documentary and 'genre', made up of highly evocative and effective elements. Elements of this drawing, in some of the groups of Arabs, are to be found in his paintings of Egyptian subjects, especially in his *Caravan at Rest* of 1844 (Perocco, 1979, no. 81).

Artists' Biographies

A

Jacopo Amiconi (Naples 1682-Madrid 1752) received his early training in the Neopolitan milieu of Solimena. Shortly afterwards, he moved to Venice and took up the legacy of Ricci and Pellegrini, lightening the sculptural quality of his figures and rising to a dazzling brilliance of colour. His pastoral subjects and the gracefulness of his Rococo taste put him among the most prominent and sought-after painters in Europe. He worked in Munich between 1717 and 1727, in London in 1729, in Paris in 1736 and again after 1739, where he reached his full maturity. In 1747 he left for Spain as the court-painter to Ferdinand VI.

Amiconi was skilful in pastoral and in portrait painting, in which he shows a typically precious, *recherché* style of drawing and a delicately-shaded palette; in his historical paintings and frescoes, he fell into a smooth, empty, almost Neoclassical style, while always preserving an elevated air of decorative dignity. Apart from his characteristic portraits, he left a few drawings of a soft and velvety treatment.

Guiseppe Angeli (Venice 1712-1798) is the best-known of Piazzetta's Venetian followers, and appears from an inscription on a painting of 1745 to have been the Director of the *Bottega*. Most of his numerous paintings are in Venetian churches, in the Ospedaletto (1748), the Pietà (1754) and in the Palazzo Pisani Moretta. His delicate and gauzy style softens Piazzeta's sturdy anatomy with the purest Rococo touches. His drawings also retain certain delicate pastel shades, which were highly appreciated by collectors, although on poetic grounds they are much less worthy than those of his master.

Andrea Appiani (Milan 1754-1817) was trained in the Milanese circle of the newly-founded Accademia di Brera after an initial apprenticeship in the studio of Carlo M. Giudici.

He became a freemason at an early age, and was friendly with the whole of the enlighted and reformist circle in Lombardy, from Parini to Piermarini, Aspari, Monti, Foscolo and Albertolli, becoming one of its most established and significant artists. He produced many paintings on a variety of sacred and secular subjects, both in fresco and in oil. Above all, he painted decorations for the palaces and villas of the best Milanese society.

He was highly regarded and enjoyed official positions and recognition during the Napoleonic era, when he was, so to speak, the official portraitist and court-painter, and, from 1802, the General Commissioner for the Fine Arts. Appiani produced cycles of decorative paintings in praise and celebration of Bonaparte, but also painted a vast output of private and informal works, of high quality and repute. In both of these styles he managed to express a Neoclassicism that had been matured by the influence of the most recent and advanced artistic achievements of French culture, no less than by his studies and enthusiastic researches into early Renaissance painting in Lombardy and the Po Valley. Most of his work is to be found in the region of Lombardy: his great fresco decorations on mythological and allegorical themes are the best-known and appreciated of all his work.

B

Marcantonio Bassetti (Verona 1586-1630) was a pupil of F. Brusasorci, and studied the work of Tintoretto in Venice. Afterwards he moved to Rome and elaborated a style of painting with a densely-toned impasto that was the hallmark of Caravaggio. Returning to Verona in around 1620, he produced some remarkable portraits inspired by Bassano, such as the *Old Man with a Book* in the Museum of Castelvecchio.

Guiseppe Bazzani (Mantua 1690-1769) was evidently influenced in his training by Rubens' paintings in Mantua, and also by the great Venetian tradition from Tintoretto and Veronese (the *Annunciation* in the Brass Collection in Venice) to Maffei (*Scenes from the Life of Alexander the Great* in the Palazzo d'Arco in Mantua). Besides his fluid colours and the elegant chiaroscuro that characterize his early work, his mature paintings display qualities of soft modelling and a prevalence of curving lines in a clearly Rococo taste (*St. Thomas writing before the Cross*, Palazzo Ducale, Mantua; *Vision of St. Romualdo*, Chiesa di San Barnaba, Mantua). These elements confirm his recognizable links with contemporary European painting, from Guardi to Watteau and Fragonard.

Bernardo Bellotto (Venice 1721-Warsaw 1780) began his career in Venice, at the studio of his uncle, Antonio Canal, in 1738-43, when his name was enrolled in the Fraglia. He left Canaletto's studio in 1744-45 and moved to Lombardy; from 1747 to 1759 he was in Dresden, then in Vienna from 1759 to 1760, in Munich in 1761 and again in Dresden between 1762 and 1767. Eventually in 1767 he went to Warsaw, where he remained until his death. It is hard from the start to distinguish the style of Bellotto from that of Canaletto, with whom he is still confused. His paintings in Turin and Varese are undoubtedly his own work, and allow us to recognise his typical *verismo*, and the precise linguistic characters that distinguish him from his uncle: a more strongly accented chiaroscuro, the cold tonality of his light blues, his pedantic minuteness of detail, and a uniform palette that rarely uses a mixture of tones. His many drawings are to be found in Darmstadt and Warsaw.

Federico Bencovic (?Dalmatia *c.* 1677-Gorizia 1756). After his training in Emilia, which began around 1695 with Cignani in Bologna, and continued into the first decade of the eighteenth century with Crespi, Bencovic went back to Venice, where he remained between 1710 and 1716. Here he seemed particularly impressed by Piazzetta's dramatic chiaroscuro, which he interpreted in a restless manner in his paintings in the Castel of Pommersfelden, with dark colours streaked with flashes of light. In 1716 Bencovic was in Vienna, where he stayed for about ten years, attracting members of the young Austrian school towards Venetian painting, from Troger to Zink and from Maulpertsch to Kremser Schmidt. On returning to Venice, he probably painted the Gambacorti altarpiece in San Sebastiano, which shows still greater contrasts of light and shade, while the small altarpiece in Borgo San Giacomo, possibly painted after 1730, already shows a closer approach to the manner of Ricci and of Tiepolo himself. In 1733 and 1743 Bencovic was in Vienna, and eventually went from there to Gorizia. His few surviving drawings show early affinity to the Emilian style, and later to that of Piazzetta.

Giovanni Carlo Bevilacqua (Venice 1775-1849) studied at the Accademia dei Pittori from 1788 to 1791, where he was Professor of Life Drawing from 1801 to 1804. He also carried out public commissions as a restorer. He frescoed various rooms in the new Palazzo Reale (formerly the Procuratie Nuove and the Biblioteca di San Marco) and in various houses; he worked on portraits and religious paintings, and also excelled in graceful and elegant decoration in the Neo-Pompeian, grotesque, allegorical and historical narrative styles, on clearly Neo-classical lines. Bevilacqua worked mainly in the Veneto – in Venice, the Villa Pisani at Stra, Trieste, Padua, Mira etc. – and is a good representative of the taste that spread after the fall of the Republic and with the advent of the French and the triumph of Neoclassicism. He worked for many years but with little financial satisfaction, and attempted repeatedly but without success to get himself appointed as a curator in the Venetian museums and galleries.

Guiseppe Bernardino Bison (or Bisson) was born in Palmanuova – now in the province of Uldine – in June 1762: his mother was Venetian and his father came from Treviso. His family moved to Brescia where he had his first training, but soon he established himself in Venice, where, due to his evident gifts as an artist, he attended the Accademia di Pittura for ten years. He was taught by C. Cedini and A. Mauro, but was also influenced by his acquaintance with all the major late eighteenth-century Venetian artists and watching them at work: from Guardi to the Longhis, from Marieschi to Guarana, while he learnt the technique of fresco from Cedini. He worked in Venice (where he was also a scene-painter at the La Fenice Theatre), and in Trieste, Gorizia, Zara, Ferrara, Treviso and Milan, where he remained for many years, and died in August 1844 at the end of a career as a painter that was richly productive, if economically unrewarding.

Bison mingled echoes of eighteenth-century Venice in his works, often ironically filtered with suggestions derived from the years of crisis and the profound transformations of the Napoleonic era, and lastly, with the themes and sensibilities established by Romanticism.

Guiseppe Borsato (or Borsatto) was born in Venice in 1770, the son of Marco, who was also a sculptor. He attended the Accademia di Pittura in 1791-92 under the direction of the perspective painter Gerolamo Mengozzi Colonna. In Rome, he entered Canova's circle, and settle in Venice in the Napoleonic era and during the Habsburg era that followed, as the greatest exponent of ornate Neoclassical painting. Borsato was the official scene-painter to the Fenice Theatre, and also often directed great public festivities by planning stage-effects and impromptu celebratory works. He was a great decorative painter in the French style of Percier and Fontaine, and painted ceilings and scenery for various theatres, working several times in the Fenice Theatre in Venice, in the Teatro Nuovo in Padua, the Udine theatre and in the Teatro Vendramin in Venice.

As a decorator, ornamenter, designer and planner of furniture and interiors, (in the Palazzo Reale in Venice, for example), and as the Professor of Ornament at the Academy of Fine Arts, Borsato was the most representative figure, together with Selva and Santi, of the various phases of Neoclassical taste in Venice. He also painted views and historical paintings, without managing to go beyond the quality and effectiveness of his ornamental work.

Mattia Bortoloni (San Bellino Polesine 1696-Milan 1750) started his career, according to Zanetti, under the guidance of Balestra. He was enrolled in the Fraglia dei Pittori in 1720, and again between 1726 and 1734, working mostly in the Veneto, at the Villa Cornaro in Piombino Dese (1716), at Tolentini in Venice (1732) and in Piedmont, where he painted the frescoes in the Santuario di Vicoforte in Modovi in 1748. Recent work has shed light on Bortoloni,

who was one of the most interesting personalities in the early eighteenth-century Veneto. Bortolini drew upon the more daring seventeenth-century sources, from Carpioni to Maffei, and shows a typically Baroque language of decoration, bringing it up to date, without any loss of vivacity, through his Tiepolesque handling of light. However, his style of drawing still remains bound to that of Celesti and Ricci.

Eugenio Bosa (Venice 1807-1875) was the son of Antonio Bosa, a sculptor of modest talents in the Canovan style, and began work as a sculptor himself. He moved on to drawing and painting, and was so prolific and enjoyed such good fortune with the public that he was able to retire at the age of forty and live off the income from his earnings.

He was a facile painter and an instinctive illustrator, and concentrated above all on genre scenes, and typical occurrences of everyday life, paying great attention – in an absolutely superficial manner, however – to the living-conditions and habits of the poorest classes. Many of his works were also engraved, and were widely distributed.

Gerolamo Brusaferro (Venice 1680-1760). His enrolment in the Fraglia identifies his presence in Venice between 1702 and 1721; his altarpiece in the Chiesa di Santo Stefano in Venice dates from 1737. He is remembered as a pupil of Bambini, and seems somewhat influenced by Ricci, imitating his sense of composition without managing to approach his richness of colour. His drawings are lighter and more airy, in the manner of Pellegrini.

C

Ippolito Caffi (Belluno 1809-Lissa 1866) is the best of the nineteenth-century Venetian view-painters. After an initial apprenticeship in the provinces, he was trained at the Academy of Fine Arts in Venice, where he was taught by Tranquillo Orsi, Francesco Bagnara and Teodoro Matteini. He travelled continuously in Europe and the Near East, and made a number of important visits to Greece, Egypt and Nubia; he took part in many of the nationalist and anti-Austrian movements in Veneto, Rome and in Friuli, and died in a naval engagement between the Italians and the Austrians at Lissa in 1866. Caffi was a romantic both in his attitude to life and in his choice of artistic subjects, always remaining faithful to the view-painting tradition, in which he established himself with a huge collection of works which take their subjects from all the countries the artist visited.

Caffi enriches his views with a great emotional involvement, which he expresses in the frequency and intensity of highly-charged and picturesque atmospheric conditions, painting sunsets, effects of moonlight, eclipses, snow and mist etc.

In this respect, and in the wake of some of Guiseppe Borsato's landscapes, Caffi shows a desire to transfer the attention of the view-painters to scenes that are related to psychological conditions and states of mind in the way they convey magical and exciting atmospheres, both in the more clearly orientalized examples of Egyptian and Palestinian scenes executed in strongly-coloured inks, and in the more peaceful and meditative Venetian, Ligurian and Piedmontese scenes.

Carletto Caliari (Venice 1570-1596) was the son of Paolo Veronese, and worked as one of his assistants with his brother Gabriele and his uncle Benedetto. Besides his few paintings, he is noted for a series of portraits in coloured pastel, which show a careful and detailed style that is close to the manner of Bassano, whose pupil he had been.

Luca Cambiaso (Moneglia 1527-Madrid 1585) worked first of all in Genoa, then moved to Madrid in 1583. As a young man he had been influenced by the gigantic figures of Michelangelo and Pordenone (Palazzo Doria in Genoa); but afterwards he clarified and loosened his style through his knowledge of the Venetian painters and of Correggio. His many drawings, with their dynamic composition, are exceptionally brilliant and incisive.

Antonio Canal (known as Canaletto) (Venice 1697-1768) was the son of a scene-painter, and worked initially in the theatre in Venice and Rome, but after 1719, returning to Venice, he turned entirely towards view-painting, taking the topography, festivities and architectural caprices of Venice as his subjects. Initially, he followed Marco Ricci in painting ruins, and then Carlevaris in his balanced rectilinear perspectives. Smith, the English Consul, became his patron, and the rich Englishmen passing through Venice became his principal clients. Among those who ordered views of Venice by the dozen were the Duke of Buckingham (in the Harvey Collection in Birmingham), the Duke of Bedford (whose paintings are still at Woburn Abbey) and Smith himself, whose pictures are in Windsor Castle. He worked in England from 1746 to 1755, leaving many masterpieces including the *Views of Oxford* in the National Gallery in London, before returning to Venice where, after being elected belatedly to the Academy, he died. Draughtsmanship took up much of Canaletto's life, in the series of thirty-five etchings he made for Smith between 1741 and 1744, and in his drawings, of which some hundreds are known. Half of these are kept at Windsor.

Antonio Canova (Possagno, Treviso 1757-Venice 1822) is certainly the greatest Italian artist of the Neoclassical era, and one of its most complete and influential representatives on the Continent.

Canova was trained in Venice, where he showed the first signs of his exceptional quality as a sculptor; when barely twenty-two years old, he moved to Rome, which was recognised as the artistic capital of Europe in the years that spanned the late eighteenth and early nineteenth centuries.

He combined the study and practice of the antique with a careful observation of the classical direction in which art was being reformed, and with an acquisition of all the fundamental problems of Neoclassicism in the wide and varied Romantic universe.

Canova was an artist of great sensitivity and refinement, and his works are infused with an agonizingly poetic delicacy, soon to become the very incarnation of the ideal of grace, formal perfection and intellectual and literary richness that give the most complete and coherent explanation of the word 'Neoclassical', and almost becoming a compulsory model in every manifestation of art.

Canova was in great demand in all the European courts, and became their official portraitist, where he often put forward canons and attitudes of taste drawn more or less faithfully from the sculpture of the past. He was a valuable and well-informed painter, as well as an architect who left an important Neoclassical building, the Temple of Possagno.

Francesco Capella (Venice 1714-Belluno 1784) is regarded as the best of Piazzetta's assistants, and remained wtih him from his early youth. We find his name enrolled in the Fraglia dei Pittori in 1744; in 1757 he moved to Bergamo, where he performed an important cultural service by popularizing the style of Piazzetta.

A characteristic of Cappella is his adherence to Piazzetta at his best, during the decade between 1735 and 1745, using a dense range of colours with a mellow and sparkling tonality, as can be seen in his paintings in San Martino at Alzano Maggiore in 1749. His turning towards a richly attractive style of painting, often of a fresh and popular conception, was confirmed by his Bergamo period, where he was also influenced by Tiepolo. Cappella's delicate chromatic glazes were prepared by his graphic linedrawing, which is a little hesitant but delicately shaded.

Luca Carlevaris (Udine, 1663-Venice, 1730) came to Venice from Udine in 1679, then went on to study in Rome, returning to Venice, enriched with experience, towards the turn of the century. The Venetian countryside had attracted the interest of painters for centuries, and at the beginning of the eighteenth century, Luca Carlevaris made it the sole object of his work. Since then, views of the city in the lagoon became a popular subject, and monopolised the activity of many artists, some great ones amongst them.

Carlevaris's training was half Venetian (from Heintz) and half Roman (especially from Van Wittel); his palette was lively if somewhat crude, and his handling of perspective masterly. His views are generally realistic, but sometimes they are imaginative creations, with solemn ruins and busy riverports, and these, filled with a Romantic intensity, are among the most beautiful. Carlevaris's draughtsmanship is weak in line and rather indecisive in character. His greatest merits lay in his skilful caricatures, whose vivacious expressions are taken from life.

Andrea Celesti (Venice 1636-Toscolano, Brescia c. 1712) was a pupil of Ponzone and Mazzoni, and worked in Venice, Brescia, Lake Garda, Treviso, Asolo and Verolanuova, painting frescoes and vast canvases on religious subjects in a rich and exuberant style.

Gian Battista Crosato (Venice c. 1685-1758) apparently had his training outside Venice, as he is rather close in character to Sebastiano Ricci. Certainly, his academically articulated compositions and his somewhat cold range of colour with its changeable tonality suggest a training in Emilia or in central Italy. In any case, Crosato's first significant works are his frescoes in the Stupinigi hunting-lodge and those of the Villa della Regina in Turin, which are datable to around 1733. There is some reference to the Venetian Cinquecento tradition in his lively colours, but it is possible to detect an interpretation tending towards sculptural and even theatrical effects, in contrast to the more genuine spirit of Venetian painting. Crosato returned to Venice in 1736, making it his permanent home after 1743.

His masterpiece is the fresco in the ballroom of the Ca' Rezzonico, supposedly painted in 1753: this brilliant phantasmagoria of images shows the artist's theatrical background and his understanding of Tiepolo's silvery luminosity, that is also present in his few surviving drawings.

D

Egidio dall'Oglio (Cison di Valmarino 1705-Venice 1784) was the eldest of Piazzetta's assistants, and worked mainly in the Veneto provinces, at Cison, Castelfranco and Cornuda (Pallucchini 1955). His *Holy Family*, dated 1735, in the Duomo of Belluno, shows a strongly plastic interpretation of Piazzetta's methods, with a particularly lively palette that is close to the local tradition of Ricci and Diziani. His drawings show a great affinity with those of Piazzetta, though in a more popular style.

Jacopo da Ponte (known as Bassano) (Bassano c. 1517-1592) studied in Venice with Bonifacio dei Pitati, then returned in 1540 to his native Bassano and never moved away. In his most interesting period he came close to Mannerism, influenced by Parmigianino's prints, as we can see in his *Execution of John the Baptist* in Copenhagen, c. 1550. He developed an individual style of pastoral, with a good deal of landscape, in his various *Adorations of the Wise Men and Shepherds* (in the Ambrosiana in Vienna) which almost established the standards of an independent genre. His later works, such as the *Baptism of St. Lucilla* in Bassano, 1581, make use of an extraordinary *chiaroscuro* technique, often with nocturnal effects. This output of paintings relied on preparatory drawings, and there are many examples of these.

Gaspare Diziani (Belluno 1689-Venice 1767) was active in Venice from 1710, having previously worked in Germany, and took part in the decorative trend led by Ricci and Pellegrini, painting extensively in the churches of Venice and its territories. He was a prolific draughtsman, and a vast collection of his work, held in the Correr Museum, is considered to be among the greatest monuments to the Rococo style of drawing.

Albrecht Dürer (Nuremburg 1471-1528), the son of a goldsmith, was inspired by Schongauer's engravings, and soon devoted himself chiefly to producing copperplate engravings and woodcuts, such as the *Apocalypse* of 1498. His visit to Venice between 1494 and 1495 brought him into contact with the sources of the Renaissance. he returned to Venice in 1506-06??, and completed the *Feast of the Rosary* (now in Prague) for the church of San Bartolomeo, and a number of portraits and Madonnas. He partly adopted the influence of Bellini, but also gave the younger Venetian artists such as Giogione, Lotto and Titian, the realistic model of his own vision of nature. He returned to Nuremburg, and did not leave it again, except for a journey to Flanders in 1520.

Dürer's vast influence on the field of Western art was chiefly through his drawings and prints.

F

Francesco Fontebasso (Venice 1709-1769) was a pupil of Sebastiano Ricci, and was familiar with the artistic circles of Bologna and Rome, attempting to establish a bond with the style of the greatest master of Rococo decoration, Gian Battista Tiepolo. There is always a certain sculptural heaviness at the basis of his style, which results from the Romano-Emilian influence recorded in his early years. His paintings rarely allow more than one interpretation, even though they are lively and rich in chromatic spontaneity, and fluent in form. He had a successful career, also working in Trento and for the Russian court, where he stayed in 1760-62.

Fontebasso was particularly successful in smaller paintings, and in his *modelli*, where his instinct for colour overcame the difficult combination of Ricci and Tiepolo by arriving at expressions of a hearty, almost vulgar vitality. In his drawings, of which there is a remarkable collection in the Correr, he is closer to Ricci than to Tiepolo.

G

Antonio Gaspari (Venice *c.* 1660-Castel Guglielmo (Rovigo) ? between 1738 and 1749) is one of the most interesting architects of the late-Baroque.

He was in the service of a number of noble Venetian families, and had a particularly close connection with the Morosini: the family's chief representative, the celebrated Doge Francesco, conqueror of the Peloponnese, gave Gaspari the job of superintending the work on the Palazzo di Santo Stefano.

Although Gaspari was a collaborator and follower of Longhena on many occasions, he cannot be called a faithful interpreter, since he showed an inclination towards the Romano-baroque, which he also proposed as a model for Venice to adopt. Gaspari reconstructed and modernized many of the oldest buildings in Venice, and also planned some important architectural works of his own, the most important being the Palazzo Zenobio ai Carmine, the great Morosini arch in the Doge's Palace, the church of S. Maria della Consolazione (known sa *la Fava*) and the Este Duomo.

Pier Leone Ghezzi (Rome 1674-1755) worked in an eclectic manner as a painter, chiefly of frescoes, which he executed in several Roman churches and, with better results, in the Villa Falconieri at Frascati in 1727, where he drew scenes of contemporary life. His reputation rests on his rich series of drawings, including an exceptionally good-natured group of caricatures of the society of his time.

Nicola Grassi (Formeano 1682-Venice 1748) was trained in the provinces, but this did not greatly influence his personality as an artist. He was inspired early on in his career by the rich and pithy paintings of Carneo, but his move to Venice, where he remained until 1721, was decisive. These ten years brought Grassi into contact with the various tendencies of the group around Piazzetta and Bencovic, as well as with the lighter and much more decorative manner of the creators of the Rococo, from Ricci to Pellegrini.

From 1731 onwards (the date of the Endenna altarpiece), Grassi came still closer to the clarity of Pellegrini, with results that approach those of his contemporary, Gian Antonio Guardi. In the series of *Apostles* and of the altarpieces for the Duomo of Tolmezzo in the 1740s, he came close to the style of his fellow-countryman Pittoni, in a gracefully Rococo version of the brilliant compositional invention of his youth. His few surviving drawings begin in the manner of Ricci, and later become lighter and more irregular.

Jacopo Guarana (Verona 1720-Venice 1808) is admired along with Giambattista Tiepolo as a decorator of Venetian churches and palaces in the second half of the eighteenth century. Among other works, he painted the frescoes in the cupola of the Basilica di San Vitale in Ravenna; those in the Ospedaletto the Ca' Rezzonico and the Doge's Palace in Venice, and others in the Villa Pisani at Stra. He was certainly trained in the manner of Ricci, but after the middle of the century he assimilated some of Tiepolo's crystalline luminosity. His fluent and sinewy drawings are often confused with those of Diziani.

Francesco Guardi (Venice 1712-1793) was a younger brother of Gian Antonio, and worked with him in his studio until around 1740, copying pictures and producing decorative and religious paintings. Then, when Canaletto left for England, he took over from his as a view-painter, and afterwards concentrated almost exclusively on this style of painting. In the 1770s, he produced the series of twelve *Feste ducale* taken from the prints of Canaletto and Brustolon, most of which are preserved in the Louvre, and in 1782 he was commissioned by the Venetian Republic to record the state visit of the Grand Dukes of Russia (the *Concerto di dame* in Munich) in a style that was distinguished from Canaletto's by its sinewy freedom of line and its capricious imagination. Guardi was a prolific draughtsman, and prepared his paintings with general sketches and extraordinarily evocative details, with short, broken pen or brush strokes, and also prepared larger drawings for connoisseurs. The largest collection is in the Correr Museum in Venice, and has come down to us directly from the artist's son.

Giacomo Guardi (Venice, 1764-1835) was the son of Francesco, and perpetuated his father's style, reducing his subjects of Venetian views to a mere production of genre-paintings for tourists. Apart from his rare canvases, such as the *Island in the Lagoon* in the Gallerie di Venezia, he mainly produced small, coloured tempera-drawings on paper, in at least three formats up to quarto size, sometimes tinted a pleasant bluish-pink, and with a detailed if awkward style of drawing. His pen-drawings, kept in large numbers in the Correr Museum, also plagiarise his father's subject-matter, even though they are clearly distinguished stylistically by his turning towards the cold documentary light of Canaletto's followers.

Gian Antonio Guardi (Vienna 1699-Venice 1761) belonged to a family of painters, together with his younger brothers Francesco and Nicolo. His father Domenico was also a painter, living in Vienna at the end of the seventeenth century, but none of his paintings are known to survive. When Domenico moved to Venice and shortly afterwards died, Gian Antonio took over his studio, and was his brothers' first master. Together with them he initially devoted himself to copying famous works by Tintoretto, Ricci and Piazzetta, and family portraits commissioned by the famous collector Marshal Schulemburg. Later he came into contact with the best artists of the Venetian Rococo, particularly Sebastiano Ricci, Pellegrini and Tiepolo, who married his sister Cecilia. From the beginning of the 1740s, Gian Antonio painted some real masterpieces in the Rococo style, that are exceptional for their lightness of touch and their fluttering airiness of colour, such as the *Stories from Gerusalemme liberata* in the National Gallery of Washington, and the *Aurora* in the Cini collection in Venice. But Gian Antonio's masterpiece remains the organ-chancel in the Chiesa dell'Angelo Raffaele in Venice, with its edgy, darting brushstrokes, in a style that already prefigures the sunny palette of Turner. We know of about a hundred drawings by Gian Antonio, in which he constructs a freer manner of Rococo painting upon the foundation laid by Ricci.

H

Francesco Hayez (Venice 1791-Milan 1882) passed through practically all the stages of nineteenth-century painting and art during the course of a long and active life. He learnt the first rudiments of painting from Francesco Maggiotto, a late follower of Piazzetta, and soon entered the Venetian cultural circle that was inspired, from Rome, by Antonio Canova. He came into contact with various painters of an academic stamp such as Querena and Matteini, and was definitely able to drop any suggestion of the eighteenth century. In Rome, where he was in contact with Canova from 1809, he fully acquired the linguistic tools and cultural baggage of the Roman Neoclassical world, without neglecting his study of Raphael and the early Cinquecento. He stayed in Venice from 1817 to 1822, and eventually settled in Milan after 1823, where he held the Chair of Painting at the Accademia di Brera, and from there he took part successfully in a large number of shows and exhibitions in Italy and abroad.

Hayez was a very effective painter in his Neoclassical period, and also in his subsequent career as a historical and patriotic painter. He is now also admired as a painter of portraits, although these became progressively marked by the varnished and commemorative official manner that his clients admired.

Hayez was capable of grandly evocative and emotionally arousing work, and was gifted with an astonishing pictorial technique. However, he was often bookish and cold, while on other occasions he turned to his own rich repertoire of preconstituted emotions and was rhetorically equipped for the virtuoso resolution of difficult pictorial problems.

As a first-rate exponent of Risorgimento painting, Hayez did not abandon his function as the painter of the court and the reigning family, nor, on other occasions, the painting of genre scenes.

K

Anton Kern (Tetschen, 1709-1747) was a member of a large family of painters, and had his initial training in Bohemia, moving to Venice in 1725, where he frequented Pittoni's studio for about a decade. It is certain that he returned to Prague in 1735, when he was enrolled in the University there. Kern's paintings are often copied from those of Pittoni, like the *Saint Elizabeth* in Prague and the *Sacrifice of Polyxena* in Litomerice, and he principally concentrated his interest in working out a number of drawings, which are also easily confused with those of his master. His style is distinguished by his thicker and dryer shading, which loses the delicate pictorial effects of Pittoni's originals.

L

Gregorio Lazzarini (Venice, 1665-Villabona Veronese, 1703) was an elegant and self-confident decorative painter, with a lively feeling for colour and a grandiose sense of composition. He painted decorations in S. Pietro di Castello, *Allegories* in the Sala dello Scrutinio in the Doge's Palace in Venice. His paintings influenced his young pupil, G.B. Tiepolo.

Pietro Longhi (Venice 1702-1785) was trained in the school of Balestra, and left some early works of little value, that indicate his lack of inclination towards the grand style of decorative painting. A visit to Bologna in around 1730 brought him into contact with the intimate, lively manner of Crespi. After this, he devoted himself to painting conversation-pieces, portraying Venetian society in all its public and private aspects. With their extraordinary stylistic consistency, his little paintings give us the most faithful image of his time. His drawings are particularly interesting, and show connections with the international taste for the French style of conversation-piece. Most of these drawings are now in the Correr Museum, where they were purchased directly from his son Alessandro, who was also a painter and a well-known portraitist at the end of the eighteenth century.

Johann Carl Loth (Munich 1632-Venice 1698) was a German painter who based himself in Venice around the middle of the seventeenth century, and gained a wide success through his vividly naturalistic paintings, which show the influence of the local tradition and of the style of Caravaggio such as the *Jupiter and Mercury entertained by Philemon and Baucis*, Vienna. His style later became calmer and clearer, possibly under the influence of Maratta, as can be seen in the altarpiece in S. Maria del Giglio in Venice.

M

Francesco Maffei (Vicenza *c*. 1600-Padua 1660) was trained in Vicenza in the milieu of late Mannerism, and followed the tradition of the great Venetian masters of the Cinquecento. Later, he became influenced by the painters of the Venetian revival, such as Liss, Fetti and Strozzi. His work falls between the disquiet of Mannerism and the exuberance and imagination of the Baroque, in his *Allegory of Alvise Foscarini* in the Vicenza Museum, *The Adoration of the Magi* in the Duomo, Vicenza, *The Translation of the Saints* in the Duomo Vecchio in Brescia, and the series of *The Miracles of St Nicholas* in S. Nicola, Vicenza.

Gian Battista Marcuola (Verona 1711-1780) was a prolific artist, many of whose works are to be found in the churches of Verona, where he also taught at the Accademia di Pittura. He is mentioned in the records as a pupil of Simone Brentana, but appears from his numerous drawings to be more closely connected with the Venetian manner of Ricci. As a draughtsman, he shows a fine knowledge of Venetian drawing, and uses a style of pictorial relief, with dashes of water-colour on a linear background that preserves a certain fluidity of drawing that was typical of Celesti.

Gerolamo Mauro II (Venice 1729-1766) was the son of Alessandro, according to the Fraglia dei Pittori. As with the two Antonios of the same family, it is difficult to distinguish the activities of the two Gerolamo cousins, who worked simultaneously and sometimes in collaboration in the same theatres, until 1766, the year of Gerolamo II's death. He was described in the *Notatori Gradenigo* as being 'the chief among Venetian theatrical painters, in which field he brought honour on himself and on his family through his achievements in producing scenery and marvellous contrivances for the stage. Ultimately he was given the position of Superintendent to the great task of organizing the *Peattoni Ducali* and the magnificence of the first promised the grandeur and inventiveness of the other two, which were even more splendid and elegant. He died at the age of 41'. Two years previously, Gerolamo had collaborated with his cousin of the same name in the *Festa dell'Adrio*, a regatta held in honour of Edward Augustus, Duke of York. His theatrical work is often confused with that of Gerolamo III, and his style belongs to the greatest tradition of Rococo decorative painting.

Andrea Michieli (known as Andrea Vicentino) (Vicenza 1539/42-Venice 1614/17) was a follower of the Venetian painters of the second half of the sixteenth century, in particular of Tintoretto, and worked on the decoration of the Doge's Palace.

N

Jacopo Negretti (known as Palma the Younger) (Venice 1544-1628) was the great-nephew of Palma the Elder, and had his early training in Urbino and Rome, which directed him towards the current of Mannerism. He came back to Venice in 1570 as an assistant to Titian, and after the death of the great masters, he assumed the position of a general-purpose painter, working in the Doge's Palace, the Oratorio dei Crociferi (from 1583 to 1591), in the School of San Fantin and in innumerable other secular and religious buildings. He was an inexhaustible draughtsman, and left thousands of drawings, which are often still bound up in small volumes (such as those in Munich and London), intended for study and for the preparation of paintings.

Guiseppe Nogari (Venice 1699-1763) has been unjustly neglected by modern criticism, but enjoyed a considerable reputation in his time, and worked throughout the Veneto, in Milan and at the Royal Palace in Turin. He was among the founders of the Accademia di Pittura in 1756, and became its president in 1762-63.

Nogari is traditionally regarded as a pupil of the great *compositore* Antonio Balestra, but he does not display a grand style in his major paintings, where instead he seems to follow Piazzetta in a certain sunny softness of tone. His pastel-drawings and his acquaintance with Rosalba Carriera led him to concentrate on portraiture and character-studies, inspired (after Nazzari's example) by the manner of Rembrandt. Some of his pastels and tinted drawings achieve subtle tonal effects, with an evanescent musical quality.

Pier Antonio Novelli (Venice, 1729-1804) went, after an early stay in Venice, to Bologna in 1773 and to Rome in 1779, where he stayed at intervals until the end of the century. Besides his numerous canvases, he also painted frescoes at Padua and in Friuli. Novelli passed during his long working life thorough the consecutive experiences of the eighteenth century. Initially, he looked towards the freer and more picturesque Rococo painters like Gian Antonio Guardi and Amiconi; then, after his experience in Bologna and Rome, he declined into painting

sentimental conceits of sugary Neoclassicism. A large collection of his lively and
brilliant drawings is held in the Correr
Museum.

P

Bernardo Parentino (Parenzo, *c*. 1437-1531)
is known from his painting of *Christ Carrying
the Cross*, signed 'Bernadin Parenzan', in the
Estense Gallery in Modena. He was the son
of the painter Giovanni Parentino, and
possibly served as an Augustinian monk in
Padua, where M. Michiel attributes the
frescoes in the cloisters of Santa Giustina,
painted between 1489 and 1494, to his hand.
His training, between Mantegna and
Ferrara, is shown above all in his characteristic incisiveness of style that is evident
even in the rare drawings attributed to
him.

Gian Antonio Pellegrini (Venice 1675-1741)
set off on his travels to study in Florence,
Rome and Naples, following in the footsteps
of Sebastiano Ricci, and adopting the
graphic self-confidence and colouristic verve
of the early masters of the Rococo, especially
that of Luca Giordano. He was in England
from 1708 until 1713, and then went to
Holland, Germany and Paris (1714-1720)
where he brought the message of the new
language of decoration, supported by his
fertile production of drawings, in which we
find the origins of the more sparkling
Rococo.

Sante Peranda (Venice 1566-1638) was
brought up in the sphere of late Mannerist
painting, and was strongly influenced by
Palma the Younger. He was active in Venice,
in the Veneto region and in Emilia, where he
stood out as a painter of portraits (like that of
Giulia d'Este in the Ducal Palace in Mantua)
and of religious subjects, painted in the
School of S. Giovanni Evangelista in
Venice.

Gian Battista Piazzetta (Venice 1683-1754)
was at first a pupil of his father, a sculptor,
and was influenced from the start by the late
seventeenth-century group of Venetian
painters known as the *tenebrosi*, such as
Zanchi and Langetti. These impressions
were confirmed by his stay in Bologna where
he apparently got to know the work of
Guercino and Crespi. He appears in Venice
in the early 1720s, with his painting in San
Stae and the ceiling in San Zanipolo. He then
formed a studio of his own, incorporating
Angeli, Maggiotto, Cappella and others, and
worked successfully in Venice, where he

maintained a traditional stance in the face of
the unbridled decorativism of the Rococo,
and of the brilliant works of Tiepolo. He
became increasingly academic in the distribution of his drawings and studio engravings, and in 1750 he founded a school of
painting that was to be perpetuated by his
followers. His best works are in a more
popular and realistic vein, like the *Fortune-
Teller* in the Gallerie di Venezia, that frees
itself from the weight of late-Baroque
tradition and points the way towards modern
realism.

Giambattista Piranesi (Mogliano, Venice
1720-Rome 1778) was trained, mainly in
architecture and technical engineering, in
the Venetian offices responsible for the
coastal defences of the lagoon, and above all
by his contact with Tommaso Temanza.
However, he moved to Rome as a young
man, drawn there by the myth of the cultural
and artistic greatness of the Roman spirit of
classicism, which always remained his ideal
in his work as an engraver, as well as in his
passionate participation in theoretical
debates about architecture.
Piranesi was regarded as the chief inspiration to the *visionari* movement in art and
architecture, and held an enormous influence over all the most advanced aesthetic
and even theoretical research, through his
artistic evidence and production, handled in
a taut and radical manner that revoluti-
onised the language of engraving. Piranesi
produced a collection of engravings that bear
an archaeological stamp, and other designs
and imaginative compositions that struc-
turally introduced the theme of the *capriccio*,
bringing it to the limits of a profound
involvement in the dreams and preoccu-
pations of the eighteenth century: he often
surpasses the limitations and boundaries of
illuminism and of his own more formal
aesthetic manner, in his agonized,
sulphurous, heroic, Titanically negative
visions of history and human destiny.
Although only one of his architectural
designs – the little church of S. Maria del
Priorato on the Colle Aventino in Rome –
was ever actually built, Piranesi never
renounced his own origins, continuing until
his death to sign himself *architetto veneto*.

Gian Battista Pittoni (Venice 1687-1767)
was probably a pupil of Balestra, who directed him towards a sculpturally decorative
style, close to that of Bencovic. These aspects
of Pittoni's stylistic language, which later
became more typically Venetian in the
elegant and rather affected manner of late
Ricci, were particularly acceptable to the
taste of the mid-eighteenth century. He was

153

therefore commissioned to paint a series of altarpieces in Santa Corona, Vicenza (1723-24), at the *Santo* in Padua (1737), the Church of the Visitation in Milan (1734), in Santa Maria della Pace (1737) and San Nazario e Celso in Brescia (1740). His style became characterised by grandiose academic forms, but it did not lose the brilliant effects of his somewhat glassy chromaticism.

Today we can above all admire the fresh and witty manner of his valuable *modelletti* and his many drawings, which are among the livelier productions of the century.

Leopoldo Pollack (Vienna 1751-Milan 1806) studied in Milan as a pupil of Giuseppe Piermarini. He worked principally in Lombardy as an architect, designing buildings to private commissions, and became alienated and remote from the 'revolutionary' trends in architecture that were civically and politically drawn up in the years of democracy and later during the Napoleonic era.

Although it is in the great tradition of Neoclassicism, lively reminiscences of the International Baroque and of eighteenth-century Viennese and even Parisian styles survive in Pollack's work. These elements and attitudes can also be traced to his own personal and familiar links with the Austrian capital and with Budapest.

Pollack was very attentive and gifted in his interior design projects, and gave his best in arranging interiors in country houses (among them the Villa Belgioioso, later the Villa Reale, in Milan) and in town palaces; but he obtained equally important results in garden-architecture and in all that went with the creation and setting-out of parks with a romantic inspiration.

Q

Giacomo Quarenghi (Bergamo 1744-St. Petersburg 1817) was initially trained as a painter in Bergamo, but soon moved to Rome, where he studied with Mengs and Stefano Pazzi.

He was close to the circle of the French Academy in Rome, and here he developed his decided adherence to the rising fortunes of the Neoclassical movement. He travelled through Italy, sketching the ancient monuments and maturing a profound devotion to the teaching of Palladio. He went to St. Petersburg as the court architect to Catherine the Great, and here he remained from 1779.

Quarenghi had a vast and deserved reputation as the author of an enormous number of buildings of the most diverse purposes and dimensions, and was one of the architects who created the Neoclassical face of the Russian capital, as well as that of the peripheral but none the less interesting residences of the Tsarist court.

Quarenghi's work in designing commercial or public city buildings is of great interest and quality: in these, he moderates the more monumental and stately style of Neoclassicism and makes it more functional, in a serviceable architecture that had the typical connotations of the nineteenth-century city.

He was less influenced than others by the elaboration of Durand and his followers in the typological method of planning, but shows instead a constant tendency towards 'free' planning and towards a picturesque imagination both in his schemes for parks and open areas and in his effort to adapt himself to an urban reality.

R

Nicolas Regnier (known as Niccolo Renieri) (Maubeuge *c.* 1590-Venice 1667) was a Franco-Flemish painter who followed the Caravaggesque style of Janssens in Antwerp and that of Manfredi in Rome, and was an orthodox interpreter of the so-called *Maniera scura*. He was active in Venice from 1626, where he tempered his Caravaggesque style and came closer to the manner of the Carracci as interpreted by Reni (*The Death of Sophonisba* in the Chrysler Collection in New York, and the *Sybil* and *Judith* in the Gallerie dell' Accademia in Venice).

Marco Ricci (Belluno 1676-Venice 1730) was the nephew of the great decorative painter Sebastiano Ricci, and worked with him as a young man in the theatre, designing scenery and costumes, especially during their long visit to England from 1708 to 1712. At the same time, he was showing an increasing interest in painting ancient monuments, ruins and landscapes. He particularly devoted himself to these subjects during his stay in Rome, where he was able to study the art of the great seventeenth-century landscape-painters such as Poussin, Claude Lorrain and Salvator Rosa. His meeting with the Genoese painter Alessandro Magnasco also helped to turn him towards landscape. He returned to Venice after 1716, and devoted himself to drawing and engraving landscapes in a pre-Romantic manner that greatly interested the young Piranesi. Whole albums of drawings by Marco Ricci were recently cut up and dispersed: until then, they had preserved some of the most genuine and evocative landscape drawings of the eighteenth century.

Sebastiano Ricci (Belluno 1659-Venice 1734) made a pilgrimage between 1680 and 1706 along the itinerary of late-Baroque painting, from Bologna to Parma, Rome and Florence. After this, he developed a new pictorial language that was light and airy in colour and composition, and which formed the basis for the new language of the Rococo. He was in London from 1712 to 1715, then in Paris in 1719, and in Turin in 1724. Finally in Venice he left a series of paintings that were to be decisive in forming the new generation of eighteenth-century painters. He was a prolific draughtsman, and left whole albums of drawings that are now to be found in Venice and Windsor.

S

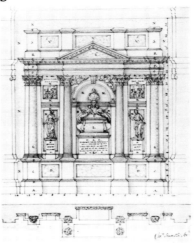

Vincenzo Scamozzi (Vicenza 1552-Venice 1616) was arguably the most prominent architect working in Venice and the Veneto after the generation of Palladio and before the success of Longhena and the Baroque era.

He was an architectural scholar and theorist, and was particularly sensitive in his response to Palladio's legacy, which he interpreted in a very personal manner, influenced by the *Libri* of Sebastiano Serlio.

Scamozzi travelled tirelessly throughout Europe, but Venice was his main centre of attraction and activity, where he obtained commissions both from the Republic and from private citizens.

In Venice itself, he was involved in the completion of Sansovino's buildings around the Piazza San Marco, and also produced many secular and ecclesiastical buildings. He was also particularly active in Vicenza, Padua and the whole of the Veneto territory, where he built villas, palaces, churches and fortifications (Palmanuova). With his contradictory and troubled personality, Scamozzi produced works that were to be held up as points of reference well into the nineteenth century, but that were also criticised for their over-casual and heretical interpretations of Palladio's teaching. Scamozzi effectively represents the turmoil, dreams and aspirations, the very delusions and difficulties of the age of transition and uneven resettling that followed the earlier serene certainties of the Renaissance.

Michelangelo Schiavone (Chioggia, active in the second half of the eighteenth century) of Dalmatian origin, was a little-known follower of Tiepolo who worked in Venice in the churches of San Giovanni in Oleo and San Geremia, and in Chioggia on the ceiling of San Francesco. When he derived his method of composition from his master, his style was easy and lively, but lost Tiepolo's colouristic values by limiting himself to a correct imitation. His interesting drawings in the Correr Museum are sometimes confused with the work of Tiepolo himself, but are identifiable by a typical hardness of line and heaviness of shading that is incapable of suggesting the values of light and colour.

Giannantonio Selva (Venice 1751-1818) was trained at the school of Tommaso Temanza. He visited Rome, where he was on friendly terms with Canova and Quarenghi among others, and travelled frequently in Europe, where he exchanged friendship and admiration with many cultural and artistic circles in various countries. Observing and taking part in the transformation of the language of architecture that was in progress during the years of his training, Selva was a convinced, if not uncritical representative of Neo-classical architecture, which he succeeded in combining with an attentive historical awareness and a minute attention to the problem of the appropriate contextualization of buildings within already existing environments.

He won the competition for the construction of La Fenice Theatre in Venice, and from that moment he enjoyed a great reputation and a position of pre-eminence among the whole architectural circle in Venice.

As the official architect in Venice during the Napoleonic era, Selva completed several projects that transformed the city at Bonaparte's request – the Giardini di Castello, Via Eugenia and the General Cemetery – which cost the city a number of serious mutilations to ancient works of art.

Selva was a refined Neoclassical architect in the French style; although he avoided abundant decoration and 'capricious' solutions, he fits in well with the tradition of Venetian 'functionalism' along the line of Lodoli-Memmo.

Francesco Simonini (Parma 1686-Venice 1753) studied at Parma with Spolverini, and showed a divergence from the manner typical of Borgognone, being influenced instead by landscape and the search for chromatic effects, which may be explained by his long stay in Venice. Through Smith's introductions, he had the best of the English aristocracy among his clients. he was also the celebrated Marshal Schulenberg's official painter, and followed him on his military campaigns.

Simonini's drawings show a great variety of style and technique. One passes from his first sketch, with its dense and dramatic effects of brushwork and its brilliant highlights, to his drawing in pen and watercolour, in a more fluent and finished style.

Bernardo Strozzi (Genoa 1581-Venice 1644) was inspired by the Baroque manner of Sorri, and showed a particular interest in the rich and magnificent paintings of Rubens and Van Dyck (Palazzo Carpaneto, Sampierdarena). He was a member of the Capuchin order, which he left on account of some obscure misadventure with the law, and fled to Venice, where he worked from 1630 until his death. There he acted as an important mediator for the Baroque, and spread his own sensual taste in coloration, both in religious paintings (*San Sebastiano* in S. Beneto) and secular works (the *Musician* in Dresden). His many drawings, often in red chalk, recall his iridescent colours and his fluid and spirited touch.

T

Bartolomeo Tarsia (Venice, known from 1711 until 1765) was the son of a sculptor, and trained among the followers of the late seventeenth-century *tenebrosa* school. He worked for a long time in Russia, where Venetian painters were welcomed in the eighteenth century. He seems to have been influenced chiefly by Molinari and Angelo Trevisani.

Tarsia's draughtsmanship was almost unknown until a signed drawing in Leningrad and four little coloured sketches in the Correr Museum for the frescoes at Peterhof were identified.

Tommaso Temanza (Venice 1705-1789) was an architect, town-planner, engineer, designer and supervisor of the *murazzi*, the sea-defences of the Venetian shoreline, an historian of Venice whose publication of the earliest map of the city is famous, and the biographer of the greatest Venetian architects from the sixteenth to the eighteenth century.

Temanza rose to a conspicuous place in the highest Venetian cultural circles, and took a middle position in the lively architectural debates of the time between the different architectural fractions, and above all between the strictest demands of functionalism of Lodoli-Memmo, the advancing studies of the Neo-Palladian language of architecture, and the technical tradition of the civil engineers and experts responsible for the great public constructions in the lagoon.

Temanza corresponded with the most notable European architectural theorists, and exerted a profound influence on a vast range of architects who refer to him explicitly as a master and an example: he is regarded today as an almost essential step in the evolution towards Neoclassicism of eighteenth-century architectural theory. Temanza designed a small number of buildings, among which the Chiesa della Maddalena is outstanding, but is better-known in the Venetian cultural panorama of his century for his writings and research.

Gian Battista Tiepolo (Venice 1696-Madrid 1770) was trained in Venice with Bencovic and Piazzetta, and then with Sebastiano Ricci; and by the 1720s he had already gained the position of an independent master. He mainly worked in fresco, in Venice, at Udine (the Archbishop's Palace and the Duomo), and then in Milan, Bergamo and Vicenza. In about 1747 he decorated the Palazzo Labia in Venice, and in 1750-53 the bishop's palace in Würzburg, which was his masterpiece. After returning to Venice to paint other canvases and frescoes, he was recalled to Stra in 1761 and to the Royal Palace in Madrid, where he remained until his death. Tiepolo's work is the most important product of the widespread Rococo style of decoration in Europe. In preparation for his frescoes, and with the aid of many studio assistants, Tiepolo produced a number of series of drawings: many volumes of these have come down to us, and they total thousands of items. It is sometimes hard to distinguish the hands of his assistants, outstanding among whom were his sons Gian Domenico and Lorenzo. Tiepolo was also very important as an engraver, and his series of *Capricci* and *Scherzi* remain among the masterpieces of eighteenth-century etching.

Gian Domenico Tiepolo (Venice 1727-1804) collaborated with his father from his earliest years, and perfectly imitated his technique, to the point of being confused with him in the authorship of his frescoes and large canvases. But at the same time he cultivated his own style, turning towards the grotesque and relying on a colder palette with characteristically chalky shades, both in his minor frescoes (like those in the guest quarters of the Villa Valmarana in Vicenza, painted in 1757) and in his smaller paintings of popular subjects, such as the *Masquerades* in the Louvre and in Barcelona. He went with his father to Würzburg and Madrid, and completed the greater part of the decorations in his family villa at Zianigo in his later years, with caricatures and carnival scenes. These frescoes were removed in about 1792, and taken to the Ca' Rezzonico. He was an active print-maker, and etched the original series of the *Flight into Egypt* and of the *Way of the Cross*: hundreds of his drawings exist, and it is often difficult to know whether to attribute them to him or to his father.

Andrea Tirali (1657-1737) was a self-taught architect who gained his knowledge through practical experience. He was drawn towards Palladio's work, both by attraction and by personal conviction, and from this point he made the first attempts at a revision of the late-Baroque architectural language, following a broadly Classical course and series of attitudes. Tirali adopted architectural novelties that often give the impression of being random quotations within buildings that are themselves difficult to classify and whose connotations seem eclectic. Some of his adaptations continue to be seen as important additions to the language of architecture, and their subsequent quotation in other buildings serves to emphasise their validity as examples. Tirali mainly worked in Venice, but there are also interesting examples of his architecture in the islands of the Venetian lagoon. His most famous works are the highly-praised Ponte dei tre Archi at Cannaregio, which is almost a textbook exercise in Palladianism; the Scuola dell' Angelo and the bell tower of SS. Apostoli, the famous porch of the Chiesa dei Tolentini, the remarkable Palazzo Venier Priuli Manfrin

on the Rio di Cannaregio, and the Chiesa dell'Apparizione at Pellestrina.

Tirali designed the paving, in white marble with a Greek key-pattern design, of the whole area around San Marco: the piazza, the piazzetta, the piazza dei Leoni and the Riva del Molo. This original piece of work was remarkably effective in defining the image of eighteenth-century Venice.

V

Antonio Vassillachi (known as Aliense) (Milos 1556-Venice 1629) was an Italian painter of Greek origin, who was a pupil of Veronese and later followed and collaborated with Tintoretto, painting (with an evident taste for the grandiose and the rhetorical) many altarpieces for Venetian churches, preparing cartoons for the mosaics in the Basilica of San Marco and participating in the decoration of the Doge's Palace.

Bonifacio Veronese (or Bonifacio de' Pitati) (Verona c. 1487-Venice 1553) was a follower of Palma the Elder in Venice, where he decorated the rooms of the Palazzo dei Camerlenghi. He was influenced by Titian's rich palette in his *Sacre Conversazioni* in the Pinacoteca Ambrosiana, the Louvre and the National Gallery of London, and also in the altarpieces in the Gallerie dell'Accademia in Venice, whereas in his subsequent works, *The Banquet at the House of Epulo* and the *Massacre of the Innocents*, in the Gallerie dell'Accademia in Venice, the *Finding of Moses* in the Brera Gallery in Milan, and *Christ among the Doctors* in the Palatine Gallery in Venice, he developed some polished and agreeable narrative gifts, setting his historical paintings in the midst of complex and evocative scenery.

Z

Guiseppe Zais (Forno di Canale 1709-Treviso c. 1784) appeared in Venice in 1748, and was enrolled in the Fraglia dei Pittori until 1768. He was a painter of landscapes and battle-scenes.

Zais was Marco Ricci's greatest follower among the Venetian landscape-painters of the eighteenth century, and he recalls his vigorous brushwork in a method of painting that is always spontaneous and brilliant. As time went by, he grew closer to the more affected style of Zuccarelli, losing his expressive intensity, but unlike the former, he still preserved a sturdy adherence to nature, seen through ingenuously Arcadian eyes.

Zais's most common drawings are those in

pen with thin watercolour. Many of these, some of them signed, are in the Correr Museum, and others are in the Albertina. In his creative phase, Zais's graphic language is characterised by his typically dry and pungent strokes, which are reminiscent of the harsher and more changeable colours of his paintings.

Antonio Zanchi (Este 1631-1722) first appears in 1666 with his paintings in the Scuola di San Rocco, inspired by the school of Ruschi, who is traditionally regarded as his teacher. He later adopted the more pictorial style of Luca Giodano, and worked in the churches of Santa Maria del Giglio, San Zaccaria and the Scuola dei Carmini.

In his eighteenth-century works, he shows the influence of Ricci's more free-and-easy style. Few of his drawings are known: one in Los Angeles and another in the Victoria and Albert Museum are characterised by a fluent if often unfocused line.

Gaetano Zompini (Nervesa 1700-Venice 1778) was introduced to the Venetian artistic milieu by his patron, A.M. Zanetti, and chiefly followed the trend set by Ricci. He deserves to be remembered more for his activity as a lively illustrator of scenes from popular life, in his series of sixty engravings of 'Le arti che vanno per via' (1753), (the original drawings are in the Correr Museum) than for the stiffly rhetorical composition of his *Bible Stories* in the School of the Carmini in Venice, painted in 1748.

Francesco Zuccarelli (Pitigliano 1702-Florence 1778) had his training in Rome under the example of landscape-painters like Locatelli and painters of ruins such as Pannini. Returning to Venice in 1732, he refined his palette, expressing it in delicate pastel shades, which made him the greatest exponent of a pictorial Arcadia that was characteristic of eighteenth-century Venice. His fame spread as a result of a journey to England, where he influenced Wilson, the great English landscape painter, and produced the *Landscapes* at Windsor. As a draughtsman, he shows an essentially

painterly touch, particularly evident in the sketchbook of the *conti* Tassi di Bergamo, which has come down to us almost intact.

Francesco Zugno (Venice, 1709-1787) was enrolled in the Fraglia dei Pittori in Venice from 1740 to 1758, and was a pupil of G.B. Tiepolo, collaborating with him on his frescoes. He also painted figures in Battaglioli's landscapes, and taught at the Accademia di Pittura from the earliest years of the institution. We can see his early work in the altarpieces of San Lazzaro degli Armeni in Venice (*c.* 1737), which still follow the style of Ricci; in the altarpieces at Cortina d'Ampezzo (painted after 1743) Tiepolo's influence is already evident. Zugno's later works, such as the *Storie Romane* formerly in the Palazzo Trento in Padua (1765), show a marked degree of academic affectation. Zugno oversweetens Tiepolo's grandiose rhetoric, and with his preciosity of drawing and his chilly refinement of colour he often comes close to the threshold of a mannered Classicism.

Bibliography

M. Abruzzese, 'Note su Pier Leone Ghezzi, in *Commentari*, 1955.

B. Aikema, 'Per Gaspare Diziani', in *Bollettino dei Musei Civici Veneziani*, 1981.

Age (The) of Neo-classicism, London, 1972.

C. Alberici, 'Disegni e stampe dell'Archivio Cagnola . . .', in *Arte Lombarda*, 1963.

K. Andrews, *National Gallery of Scotland. Catalogue of Italian Drawings*, Cambridge, 1968.

E. Arslan, 'Per la definizione dell'arte di Francesco, Giannantonio e Nicolò Guardi', in *Emporium*, 1944.

— *I Bassani*, Milan, 1960.

E. Bassi, *Giannantonio Selva architetto veneziano*, Padua, 1936.

— 'Disegni dell'Accademia di Belle Arti', in *Atti e Memorie dell'Accademia di Belle Arti di Venezia*, 1959.

— *Architettura del Sei e Settecento a Venezia*, Naples, 1962.

— 'Episodi dell'architettura veneta nell'opera di Antonio Gaspari', in *Saggi e memorie*, 1963.

R. Bassi-Rathgeb, *Un album inedito di Francesco Zuccarelli*, Bergamo, 1948.

J. Bean, F. Stampfle, *Drawings from New York Collections. The Seventeenth Century in Italy*, New York, 1967.

A. Bettagno, *Disegni e dipinti di Gian Antonio Pellegrini*, Venice, 1959.

A. Bettango, *Disegni veneti del Settecento della Fondazione Giorgio Cini e delle Collezioni Venete*, Venice, 1963.

— *Disegni di una collezione veneziana del Settecento*, Venice, 1966.

— *Le dessin vénitien au XVIII siècle*, Venice, 1971.

— *Venetian Drawings of the Eighteenth Century*, Venice, 1972.

— *Piranesi, disegni*, Venice, 1978.

A. Binion, *Antonio and Francesco Guardi*, New York – London, 1976.

— *I disegni di G.B. Pittoni*, Florence, 1983.

P. Bjurstroem, *French Drawings: Sixteenth and Seventeenth Centuries*, Stockholm, 1976.

M. Blanchard, 'Projets de monuments sur le Mont Cenis', in *Revue des Etudes Napoléoniennes*, 1917.

A. Blunt, 'Paintings by Sebastiano and Marco Ricci in the Royal Collection', in *The Burlington Magazine*, 1946.

A. Blunt, E. Croft-Murray, *Venetian Drawings of the XVII and XVIII Centuries . . . at Windsor Castle*, London, 1957.

M. Bonicatti, 'Note sul vedutismo veneziano', in *Arte Veneta*, 1964.

R. Bratti, 'Antonio Canova nella sua vita artistica privata', in *Nuovo Archivio Veneto*, 1917.

M. Brunetti, 'La laguna nell'arte e nella letteratura', in *La laguna di Venezia*, 1926.

— *Da Campoformio a Vittorio Veneto. Guida al Museo del Risorgimento*, Venice, 1952 (II ed.).

M. Brusatin, *Illuminismo ed architettura del Settecento*, Castelfranco Veneto, 1969.

— *Venezia nel Settecento: stato, architettura, territorio*, Turin, 1980.

J. Byam Shaw, 'Three Venetian Catalogues', in *Master Drawings*, 1964.

— 'Guardi Drawings', in *The Burlington Magazine*, 1976.

J. Cailleux, *Tiepolo et Guardi*, Paris, 1952.

E.A. Cicogna, *Delle iscrizioni veneziane*, Venice, 1824-53.

— *Saggio di bibliografia veneziana*, Venice, 1847.

L. Cicognara, *Storia della scultura . . .*, Venice, 1813-17.

— A. Diedo, G.A. Selva, *Le fabbriche più cospicue di Venezia . . .*, Venice, 1815-20.

E. Claye, 'A group of portrait drawings by Jacopo Amigoni' in *Master Drawings*, 1974.

L. Coggiola Pittoni, *g.B. Pittoni*, Florence, 1921.

— Disegni inediti di Giovan Battista Pittoni', in *Rivista di Venezia*, 1934.

L. Coletti, 'Restauri e scoperte. Nuovi affreschi di Gaspare Diziani', in *Bollettino d'Arte*, 1935.

W.G. Constable, *Canaletto*, Oxford, 1962.

G. Damerini, *L'arte di Francesco Guardi*, Venice, 1912.

— 'Antonio Bosa', in *Dizionario biografico degli Italiani*, Rome, 1971.

L. Dania, 'Three Drawings by Gian Antonio Guardi', in *Master Drawings*, 1966.

— 'Another Drawing by Gian Antonio Guardi', in *Master Drawings*, 1968.

G. Delogu, *Pittori Veneti Minori del Settecento*, Venice, 1930.

F. De Maffei, *Antonio Guardi pittore di figura*, Verona, 1951.

J. von Derschau, *Sebastiano Ricci*, Heidelberg, 1922.

Dessins Vénitiens, Brussels, 1983.

E. De Tipaldo, *Biografie degli Italiani illustri*, Venice, 1844.

M. Dezzi Bardeschi, 'Un monumento all'epopea napoleonica sul Moncenisio', *Psicon*, 1976 pp. 69-84.

M.V. Dobroklonsky, *Catalogue of XVII-XVIIth Century Drawings*, Leningrad, 1951.

A. Dorigato, *L'altra Venezia di Giacomo Guardi*, Venice, 1977.

R.A. Etlin, *The Architecture of death*, Cambridge, 1984.

Europäisches Rokoko, Munich, 1958.

G. Ewald, *Johann Carl Loth*, Amsterdam, 1965.

I. Fenyö, 'Disegni veneziani nel Museo di Belle Arti di Budapest', in *Acta Historiae Artium*, 1959.

G. Fiocco, *Francesco Guardi*, Florence, 1923.

— 'La pittura veneziana alla mostra del Settecento', in *Rivista di Venezia*, 1929.

— *Guardi*, Milan, 1965.

G. Fogolari, 'In tabarro e in bauta', in *Strenna dell'illustrazione italiana*, 1924-25.

M. von Freeden, C. Lamb, *Das Masterwerke des Giovanni Battista Tiepolo. Die Fresken der Wurzburger Residenz*, Munich, 1956.

M.A. Fritzsche, *Bernardo Bellotto gennant Canaletto*, Burg, 1936.

B. Gamba, *Galleria di Letterati ed Artisti*, Venice, 1842.

Giambattista Piazzetta. Disegni, incisioni, libri, Vicenza, 1983.

E. Godoli, 'Per un monumento sul Moncenisio' in *G. Pistocchi (1744-1814) architetto giacobino*, exhibition catalogue, Faenza 1974 pp. 136-142.

M. Goering, *Francesco Guardi*, Vienna, 1944.

A. Gonzales-Palacios, *David e la pittura napoleonica*, Milan, 1967.

— 'L'album del Conte Cocognara', in *Comma*, 1970.

— 'Sei fogli di Antonio Canova', in *Arte Illustrata*, 1972.

— 'I mani del Piranesi (i Righetti, Boschi, Boschetti, Raffaelli)', in *Paragone*, 1976.

D.F. von Hadeln, *Handzeichnungen von G.B. Tiepolo*, Florence, 1927.

F. Haskell, *Patrons and Painters*, London, 1963.

G. Hubert, *La sculpture dans l'Italie napoléonienne*, Paris, 1964.

— *Les sculpteurs italiens en France sous la Révolution, l'Empire et la Restauration (1790-1830)*, Paris, 1964.

Italian Drawings Masterpieces of five Centuries, Washington, 1960-61.

N. Ivanoff, *Saggio critico e catalogo delle opere del Bazzani*, Bergamo, 1950.

— 'Opere bergamasche di Mattia Bortoloni', in *Emporium*, 1957.

— 'Girolamo Pellegrini', in *Emporium*, 1958.

— 'Alcune lettere inedite di Tommaso Temanza a Pierre Mariette', in *Atti dell'Instituto Veneto di Scienze Lettere ed Arti*, 1958.

— 'Giuseppe Borsato', in *dizionario Biografico degli Italiani*, Rome, 1971.

G. Knox, *Tiepolo: a bicentenary exhibition, 1770-1970*, Cambridge, 1970.

— *Giambattista e Giandomenico Tiepolo*, Oxford, 1970.

Konstens Venedig, Stockholm, 1962.

W. Koschatzky, K. Oberhüber, E. Knab, *Grandi disegni italiani dell'Albertina di Vienna*, Milan, 1972.

H. Lapauze, D. Guarnati, 'Le paysage dans l'art vénitien du XVIII siècle, in *La Renaissance de l'Art Français*, 1919.

M. Levey, *La peinture à Venise au XVIII siècle*, Paris, 1964.

T. Locatelli, *L'appendice della Gazzetta di Venezia. Prose scelte*, Venice, 1837-1880.

E. Lo Gatto, *Gli artisti italiani in Russia*, Rome, 1934-35.

G. Lorenzetti, 'I disegni di Francesco Fontebasso', in *Rivista della città di Venezia*, 1935.

— 'Ca' Rezzonico, Venice, 1936 (I ed.).

— *Le feste e le maschere veneziane*, Venice, 1937.

— *Il quaderno del Tiepolo al Museo Correr di Venezia*, Venice, 1946.

L. Magagnato, *Catalogo della mostra dei disegni del Museo Civico di Bassano, da Carpaccio a Canova*, Venice, 1956.

— *Cinquant'anni di pittura veronese, 1580-1630*, Vicenza, 1974.

V. Malamani, *Memorie del Conte Lepoldo Cicognara*, Venice, 1888.

E. Martini, *Pittura veneta dal Ricci al Guardi*, Venice, 1977.

— *La pittura del Settecento Veneto*, Udine, 1982.

S. Mason Rinaldi, *Jacopo Palma il Giovane*, Milan, 1983.

F. Mauroner, *Luca Carlevarijs*, Venice, 1931 (II ed. 1945).

F. Mazzocca, *Invito a Francesco Hayez*, Milan, 1982.

— *Disegni neoclassici tra regola e fantasia, da Metitot a Bossi*, Florence, 1983.

G. Mezzanotte, *Architettura neoclassica in Lombardia*, Naples, 1966.

A. Mioni, 'Elementi veneti nell'architettura di Giacomo Quarenghi', in *L'Europa Orientale*, 1935.

M. Missirini, *Memorie per servire alla storia della Romana Accademia di san Luca*, Rome, 1823.

A. Morandotti, *Mostra di Giuseppe Bernardino Bison*, Venice, 1942.

A. Morassi, 'A signed Drawing by Antonio Guardi and the problem of the Guardi brothers', in *The Burlington Magazine*, 1968.

— 'Antonio Guardi as a Draughtsman', in *Master Drawings*, 1968.

— *I Guardi. Tutti i disegni di Antonio, Francesco e Giacomo Guardi*, Venice, 1975 (II ed. 1984).

L. Moretti, 'Documenti e appunti su Sebastiano Ricci', in *Saggi e memorie*, 1978.

L. Mortari, *Bernardo Strozzi*, Rome, 1966.

G. Moschini, *Della Letteratura Veneziana dal secolo XVII ai giorni nostri*, Venice, 1806.

— *Guida per la Città di Venezia . . .*, Venice, 1815.

V. Moschini, 'I disegni del Settecento alla mostra di Venezia', in *Dedalo*, 1929-30.
— *Pietro Longhi*, Milan, 1956.
— *Francesco Guardi*, Milan, 1956 (II ed.).
'Mostra di Giacomo Quarenghi a Bergamo', in *Arte Lombarda*, 1967.
A.M. Mucchi, C. Della Croce, *Il pittore Andrea Celesti*, Milan, 1954.
M. Muraro, *Disegni veneziani agli Uffizi*, Florence, 1953.

F. Nani Mocenigo, *La letteratura veneziana del secolo XIX*, Venice, 1916.
U. Nebbia, 'I disegni marinari del Carlevarijs', in *Rivista di Venezia*, 1931.
G. Nicodemi, *Appiani, 34 disegni*, Milan, 1944.

W. Oeschlin, 'Piramide et Sphère. Notes sur l'architecture révolutionnaire du XVIII siècle et ses sources italiennes', in *Gazette des Beaux Arts*, 1971.
L. Olivato, 'Temanza su Palladio: note a quattro lettere inedite', in *Odeon Olimpico*, 1970-73.
— '"Les monuments de Palladio ... font grand impression": J.A. Mariette a Tommaso Temanza', in *Arte Veneta*, 1975.
A. Ottino della Chiesa, *L'età neoclassica in Lombardia*, Como, 1959.

R. Pallucchini, 'Il pittore Giuseppe Angeli', in *Rivista di Venezia*, 1931.
— 'Antonio Marinetti detto il Chiozzotto', in *Rivista di Venezia*, 1932.
— 'Domenico Fedeli detto il Maggiotto', in *Rivista di Venezia*, 1932.
— 'Federico Bencovich', in *Rivista d'Arte*, 1932.
— 'Francesco Daggiù detto il Cappella', in *Rivista di Venezia*, 1932.
— 'Attorno al Piazzetta', in *Rivista di Venezia*, 1933.
— 'Di una pittrice veneziana del Settecento, Giulia Lama', in *Rivista d'Arte*, 1933.
— *L'arte di G.B. Piazzetta*, Bologna, 1934.
— 'Opere inedite di Giambattista Piazzetta', in *L'Arte*, 1936.
— 'Il disegno del Piazzetta per il San Giovanni Battista della Pinacoteca del Seminario di Rovigo', in *Rivista d'Arte*, 1936.
— *I disegni dei Guardi al Museo Correr di Venezia*, Venice, 1943.
— *I disegni di G.B. Pittoni*, Padua, 1945.
— *Trésors de l'art vénitien*, Milan-Brussels, 1947.
— 'Per il risarcimento della personalità del Dall'Olio', in *Arte Veneta*, 1955.
— *Piazzetta*, Milan, 1956.
— *La pittura veneziana del Settecento*, Venice-Rome, 1960.
— 'Note alla mostra del Guardi', in *Arte Veneta*, 1965.
K.T. Parker, J. Byam Shaw, *Canaletto e Guardi*, Venice, 1962.
L. Patetta, *L'architettura dell'eclettismo. Fonti, teoriche, modelli, 1750-1900*, Milan, 1980.
G. Pavanello, 'I disegni di Giovanni Carlo Bevilacqua', in *Bollettino dei Musei Civici Veneziani*, 1973.
— *L'opera completa del Canova* (intro. M. Praz), Milan, 1976.
— in *Venezia nell'età di Canova, 1780-1830*, Venice, 1978.
Peinture (la) italienne, Paris, 1960.
C. Percier, P.F.L. Fontaine, Raccolta di decorazioni interne ... con notevoli giunte di Giuseppe Borsato (edited F. Zanotto), Venice, 1843.
G. Perocco, *Ippolito Caffi*, Padua, 1979.
T. Pignatti, 'Venetian Seicento and Settecento Drawings. A Uffizi Exhibition', in *The Burlington Magazine*, 1954.

— 'Un disegno di Antonio Guardi donato al Museo Correr', in *Bollettino dei Musei Civici Veneziani*, 1957.
— 'Nuovi disegni del Piazzetta', in *Critica d'Arte*, 1957.
— 'Pellegrini Drawings in Venice', in *The Burlington Magazine*, 1959.
— 'Disegni veneti del Seicento', in *La pittura del Seicento a Venezia* (edited by P. Zampetti), Venice, 1959.
— *Il Museo Correr di Venezia. Dipinti del XVII e XVIII secolo*, Venice, 1960.
— *Eighteenth-Century Venetian Drawings from the Correr Museum*, Washington, 1963.
— *Disegni veneti del Settecento al Museo Correr di Venezia*, Venice, 1964.
— 'Nuovi disegni di figura del Guardi', in *Critica d'Arte*, 1964.
— *I disegni veneziani del Settecento*, Treviso, 1965.
— *Eighteenth-Century Venetian Drawings*, London, 1965.
— 'Il "Trionfo della Virtù Guerriera" di G.A. Guardi', in *Bollettino dei Musei Civici Veneziani*, 1967.
— *I Guardi. Disegni*, Florence, 1967.
— *Pietro Longhi*, Milan, 1968.
— *I disegni dei maestri. La scuola veneziana*, Milan, 1970.
— *La scuola veneta. I disegni*, Milan, 1970.
'La collezione Musatti di disegni antichi al Museo Correr di Venezia', in *Bollettino dei Musei Civici Veneziani*, 1970 e 1971.
— *I grandi disegni italiani nelle collezioni di Venezia*, Milan, 1973.
— *Venetian Drawings from American Collections*, Washington, 1974-75.
— 'Novità per la grafica del Celesti', in *Studi in onore di A.E. Popham*, 1980.
— 'Ancora sui disegni del Grassi', in *Nicola Grassi e il Rococò Europeo. Atti del Congresso Internazionale di Studi*, Udine, 1984.
— M.A. Chiari, *Tiziano, i disegni*, Florence, 1979.
— *Il disegno da Altamira a Picasso*, Milan, 1981.
— A. Dorigato, *Disegni antichi del Museo Correr di Venezia*, II, Venice, 1981.
— F. Pedrocco, *Disegni antichi del Museo Correr di Venezia*, III, Venice, 1983.
— F. Pedrocco, *Disegni antichi del Museo Correr di Venezia*, I, Venice, 1980.
— F. Valcanover, *18e eeuwse Venetiaanse Tekeningen*, Groningen, 1964.
G.M. Pilo, *Carpioni*, Venice, 1961.
— *Marco Ricci*, Venice, 1963.
M. Precerutti Garberi, *Andrea Appiani*, Milan, 1970.
M. Precerutti Garberi, *Giambattista Piazzetta e l'Accademia*, Milan, 1971.
L. Puppi, L. Olivato Puppi, 'Scamozziana. Progetti per la "Via Romana" di Monselice e alcune altre novità grafiche con qualche quesito' in *Antichità Via*, 1974.

C.L. Ragghianti, *Epiloghi guardeschi*, Florence, 1953.
— *Antichi disegni e stampe dell'Accademia Carrara di Bergamo*, Bergamo, 1963.
A. Ravà, *Pietro Longhi*, Florence, 1923.
A. Riccoboni, 'Antonio Zanchi e la pittura veneziana del Seicento', in *Saggi e memorie*, 1966.
F.L. Richardson, *Andrea Schiavone*, Oxford, 1980.
F. Rigon, *Disegni di Canova al Museo di Bassano*, Milan, 1982.
A. Rizzi, *Disegni, incisioni e bozzetti del Carlevarijs*, Udine, 1964.
— *Carlevarijs*, Milan, 1967.
— *Disegni del Bison*, Udine, 1976.

G.D. Romanelli, *Venezia Ottocento. Materiali per una storia architettonica e urbanistica della città nel secolo XIX*, Rome, 1977.
— in *Venezia nell'età di Canova, 1780-1830*, Venice, 1978.
— *Venezia Vienna*, Milan, 1983.
U. Ruggeri, 'Disegni di Giulia Lama al Museo Correr', in *Bollettino dei Musei Civici Veneziani*, 1973.
— 'Novità per il Piazzetta e la sua bottega', in *Critica d'Arte*, 1976.
— *Francesco Cappella detto Daggiù*, Bergamo, 1977.

L. Salmina, *Disegni veneti del Museo di Leningrado*, Venice, 1964.
Schönheit des 18. Jahrhunderts, Zurich, 1955.
F. Scolari, *Della Vita e delle Opere di Vincenzo Scamozzi ...*, Treviso, 1837.
P. Selvatico, *Sulla architettura e sulla scultura in Venezia*, Venice, 1847.
— V. Lazari, *Guida di Venezia e delle Isole circonvicine*, Venice-Milan-Verona, 1852.
Settecento (II) italiano (preface by U. Ojetti), Milan-Rome, 1932.
G. Simonson, *Francesco Guardi (1712-1793)*, London, 1904.
S. Sinding-Larsen, 'L'elemento paesistico in opere figurative dei Guardi', in *Problemi guggdeschi*, 1967.
A. Stix, L. Froelich Bum, *Die Zeichnungen der Venezianischen Schule*, Vienna, 1926.
B. Suida Manning, *Luca Cambiaso*, Milan, 1958.

T. Temanza, *Degli archi e delle volte, e regole generali dell'architettura civile ...*, Venice, 1811.
— *Lettere ...*, Venice, 1858.
— *Zibaldon* (edited by N. Ivanoff), Venice-Rome, 1963.
H. Tietze, E. Tietze Conrat, *The Drawings of the Venetian Painters in the XV and XVI Century*, New York, 1944.
P. Torriti, *Luca Cambiaso: disegni*, Genoa, 1969.

F. Valcanover, 'Un "Riposo nella fuga in Egitto" di Federico Bencovich', in *Archivio storico di Belluno, Feltre e Cadore*, 1954.
— *Ritratto veneto da Tiziano a Tiepolo*, Warsaw, 1956.
— 'Affreschi sconosciuti di Pietro Longhi', in *Paragone*, 1956.
Venezia nell'età di Canova, 1780-1830, Venice, 1978.
G. Vigni, 'La mostra udinese di disegni del Tiepolo', in *Arte Veneta*, 1965.
— *Disegni del Tiepolo*, Trieste, 1972.

P. Zampetti, *I fratelli Guardi*, Venice, 1965.
— *Dal Ricci al Tiepolo. I pittor di figura del Settecento a Venezia*, Venice, 1969.
V. Zanni, *Disegni di Giacomo Quarenghi*, Venice, 1967.
F. Zava Boccazzi, *La Basilica dei Santi Giovanni e Paolo in Venezia*, Venice, 1965.
— 'Nota sulla grafica di Antonio Kern', in *Arte Veneta*, 1975.
A.P. Zugni Tauro, *Gaspare Diziani*, Venice, 1971.